The Art of Money

by

Mike Feng Zheng

Copyright © 2022 Feng Zheng

All rights reserved. No part of this publication may be reproduced, distributed, or transmitted in any form or by any means without the prior written permission of the author.

Any references to historical events, real people, or real places are used fictitiously. Names, characters, and places are products of the author's imagination.

ISBN:

Dedication

To my father, Shide Zheng, who taught me to see the world at its full potential. My mother, BiYun Wang, was more concerned with her children than herself. My wife, Ying Chen, is my support. And to my daughters, Wendy Zheng and Willa Zheng, I am excited to grow alongside you.

Acknowledgments

The Art of Money, like any other book, would not have been able to be written without the assistance of many people who assisted me along the way. There are way too many for this to be a complete list. On the other hand, a select few have been incredibly supportive: Stella Roger and Steve Brown, who assisted me and provided direction throughout the process. Jim Kennedy is someone who inspires me, directs me, and grounds me. My wife, Ying Chen, and my daughter, Wendy Zheng, are tremendous sources of support and encouragement for me.

About the Author

Mike Feng Zheng is an entrepreneur, financier, and author. He was born in China and moved to the US in 1996. He is interested in writing books in various genres, such as investment, self-help, comics, and fantasy books. Mike Feng Zheng is currently married with two daughters. His older daughter Wendy, who is ten years old, is also an author. They live in Dallas, TX.

Contents

Introduction: How Short Life Is 1
Chapter 1: What Quantifies Success? 7
    A Part of the Rat Race 19
    What Does it Lead to Eventually? 22
Chapter 2: Corporate Slaves 25
    The African Slave 27
    Freedom of Speech in a Workplace 36
Chapter 3: Give Me Liberty or Give Me Death! 43
    The Boston Tea Party 45
    Cue the American Capitalism 46
    The Age of Industrialism 50
    History Repeating Itself 51
    Sherman's Hammer 52
Chapter 4: Financial Freedom 60
    Financial Security vs. Financial Freedom 62
        Financial Security 62
        Financial Freedom 66
        Benefits of Financial Freedom 73
        Beyond Daily Pressures 73
        Higher Fulfillment 73
        More Risks 74
    How Much Money Ensures Financial Freedom? 74
Chapter 5: Maslow's Hierarchy of Needs and Financial Freedom 79
    Growth Needs and Deficiency Needs 80
    Roadmap to Financial Freedom and Maslow's Hierarchy of Needs Model 81
    Surpassing the Rat Race 82

- Reflections on Self-Actualization 84
- Voltaire and Financial Freedom 90
- Voltaire and Passive Income 91
- Montesquieu and Financial Freedom 92
- Einstein and His Intellectual Pursuit 93

Chapter 6: 'The Simpler, The Better' Lifestyle 96
- Enter the Minimalist Lifestyle 98
- An Analysis of Consumerist and Minimalist Lifestyles 101
- Instances of Minimalist Lifestyle Adoption 104
- Steering Clear of Material Possessions 107
- The Minimalist Focus 108
- The Aim of Minimalism 110
- Minimalism Back in Childhood 110
- Putting it Into Practice 111

Chapter 7: Common Sense Investing 114

Chapter 8: The Psychology of Investing 131

Chapter 9: The All-Weather Portfolio 149

Chapter 10: The Philosophy of Real Freedom 160

Chapter 11: The Power Of Money 178

Introduction
How Short Life Is

The average life expectancy in Japan is 85.03 years, which places it in second place behind Hong Kong, which has the highest life expectancy in the world at 85.29 years. You will be astounded to find out that the United States of America only ranks # 46 with an average age of 79.11, two places after Cuba. To illustrate this chapter, let's pretend that you have the good fortune to live to the ripe old age of 82.

Now, 82 years is not an inordinate amount of time to spend in this world; however, to accomplish the purpose of this book, which is to pursue financial freedom, genuine freedom, and ultimate happiness, let's do some subtracting. The average age at which a person begins their working life is 22, and the average age at which they retire is 62. Because of this, the remainder of your working life will only be 40 years, equivalent to 14600 days or 350400 hours. The remaining years before age 62 is 116,800, calculated after deducting the eight hours per day spent sleeping.

As a consequence of this, the remainder of your working life will only span approximately 26 years. Let's conduct additional research to make something already terrible into something even worse. The findings of several studies and polls indicate that fifty percent of working Americans are dissatisfied with their jobs. This suggests that most people in the United States are unhappy with their lives because how you spend your time at work is typically how you spend your time in life. Another survey with an anonymous sample found that 85 percent of respondents were dissatisfied with their current employment situations.

There is space available for you among them because this is such a large number. Even if you don't actively despise what you do for a living, there is a good chance that you do not, at the very least, take pleasure in what you do. As a direct consequence of this, people consistently wish for the weekend and Friday evenings and look forward to them. If that's the case, it seems like the weekend is almost entirely, if not the most critical factor in determining how satisfied you are with your life.

Now, let's take your age of 26 and subtract the number of years that you've been employed from that total. There are 9500 days throughout 26 years and 260 working days each year (not counting holidays). When 6760 is subtracted from 9500, the number of days that are still available is 2740. This means that you have 7.5 years left until you reach the age of retirement, which is 62. Let's say you manage to pull yourself together over time and decide to retire when you're 62 or 65. However, in this country, the probability of acquiring a disability or mental impairment after age 65 or later is very close to as high as 70 percent. Because of this, it is doubtful that you are about to enter the joyful years of your life at this age.

Let us imagine that even if you can fully enjoy your life between the ages of 62 and 65, the risk of developing a health condition or having an existing health issue becomes significantly worse as you continue to get older. Therefore, once you retire, even if, on average, you only have 2 out of 7 good retirement days until the day you die, you will only have approximately six years of a retirement life that is both pleasurable and necessary.

In addition to that, what will happen if you have a string of unlucky weekends in a row? For instance, getting into arguments with your significant other, performing chores around the house and yard that you despise, or even staying late at work to make up for the lost time could be lousy time management. This results in an even more significant decrease in the total amount of time. If you only live your life hoping that the weekend will arrive again and again, then you wish away the majority of your existence. This is true regardless of who you are, what you do for a living, how much money you make, or the exact correctness of these numbers that I calculate.

Working at a job or for a company that does not allow you to feel enjoyable and fulfilling most of the time is the same as signing away the majority of your life. This is because most of your waking hours will be spent doing something you do not find enjoyable and that does not fulfill you. Even though it is true that there are always things that we don't want to do but have to do, it is also true that every day of our job can't be fun or how we want it to be. It won't be long before life comes to an end.

Life is still too short, even if you are fortunate enough to have a job that you take pleasure in and do not consider the number of weekdays to be time wasted. As a result, the essential thing is to make every effort to avoid irresponsibly giving up our lives. We have to be careful about what we trade it for, and we shouldn't let outside pressures like popular culture, our families, or our friends persuade us to unconsciously sell our most valuable possessions for jobs and companies that we don't genuinely enjoy and with which we don't resonate, as well as for things that we know we don't need.

When exchanging it for something else, we must watch what we give up. If you are always looking forward to the weekend, only to find that it goes by in the blink of an eye, and then you find yourself back at work on Monday wishing another weekend. This is a sign that you are truly unhappy with your lives, that you are throwing away the majority of your lives, and that you need to take a moment to stop and carefully consider what you need to do to stop wasting your lives.

The following is a chronological list of the book's chapters: In the first chapter, we discuss the factors contributing to our unhappiness. We examine them through the lens of our society's generally accepted norms of value and culture.

In Chapter 2, we discuss how we compare traditional slavery to modern forms of corporate slavery.

In Chapter 3, we discuss the idea that the notion that the United States of America is a free country is merely an illusion. What exactly should the meaning of freedom be?

Chapter 4 discusses why financial freedom is the most accurate form of liberty. The ability to control our lives and the passage of time is the most valuable commodity we can acquire.

Chapter 5 uses Maslow's hierarchy theory to demonstrate what kinds of pursuits should be considered higher or more elegant.

Chapter 6 encourage people to adopt a simpler lifestyle, such as minimalism, in exchange for increased freedom and decreased anxiety.

Chapter 7 discusses how each of us can act as our financial advisors. Why does shelling out large sums of money to hire fund managers and financial advisors will prevent you from reaching your goal of becoming financially independent? How to truly comprehend the power of compounding.

Chapter 8 uses in-depth analysis and real-world examples to illustrate how we can independently manage and grow our wealth. We cover a few key concepts that can assist you in managing your funds, acting as your financial advisor and fund manager, and managing your finances.

In Chapter 9, we discuss Ray Dalio's all-weather portfolio, which has a significantly reduced potential for loss while maintaining a satisfactory return rate over time.

In Chapter 10, we describe the concepts of the philosophy of stoicism, a wonderful preaching that many successful people have adopted throughout the history of the world for thousands of years.

Chapter 11 talks about what money is and the power of money. How can we spend money in a more meaningful way to make us happier and healthier?

Chapter 1
What Quantifies Success

Imagine you are living in a country run by a dictator. You follow a set of pre-defined rules that serve the dictator and his regime well. One step outside his rules and regulations proves to be a step in the wrong direction, with repercussions following shortly after. People are bound to this system against their will.

There is no room for free speech and free will. You are liable to bend to the will or whims of the dictator. He and his cronies run the circus at the back end, making you feel like a puppet on stage. They call the shots that you are bound to follow. And that is not all.

The dictator has a habit of demonizing other political systems. He knows what you are thinking, wishing he would fuck off at the first possible instance. The aim is to be in the good books of the people. To this end, he will begin demonizing democracy and socialism (and maybe communism), citing the failures of these political ideologies and how these systems put their people at a disadvantage. The plan is for people to rethink their existing thoughts and unlearn things that are counterproductive to the dominant regime. The dictator will go to any lengths to push this agenda, shoring up support and mass appeal for a possible next term. That is the oldest trick in the book, and it works very well as smokes and mirrors.

But demonizing the competition is not enough. It would help if you had extra reinforcements.

Cue the fearmongering. The dictator tells you about the ills of his competition and the perils of joining the other side. Press freedom will take a hit, and he will create scenarios to fuel the fire.

This is another old trick from a politician's playbook.

You may wonder what is the point of this life you have no control over? It is better to be buried six feet below the ground if life will be this way. Your friends, peers, and others live in other countries, well-off and satisfied with their standard of living.

You feel like a rat on a wheel.

You are trapped in this vicious cycle, willing to escape it at the first possible moment.

If this sounds horrible, that is because it is. Be that as it may, you are driving a car with four flat tires. You are playing cards without the ace in the hole. Take any analogy here—you are set to lose and lose big time.

Now, you may have a feeling that this system is rigged. The system is designed so that you will come out on the losing side each day of the year and possibly your whole life.

This set system is not working in your favor. However, it works very well in favor of those in the government and higher officials. Is it a fair system? You do not see it that way because the policies only work well for some people while others are at the receiving end.

Where does it all end? The system is gamed from the start —you have realized that by now. Something got to give. Agreed?

Now, I will have something to announce here. I was not talking about any dictator at all.

I was talking about capitalism!

I suggest you re-read this and see the striking similarities between the two.

Capitalism is the now-common economic system that defines success. As a system on its own, it establishes some rules to follow and changes contemporary mindsets and goals.

For the past few centuries, people have known and defined success in some ways. The notable ones involve the following:

- Success is money
- Success is fame and fortune
- Success is power

I will talk about the success that people look for in money. Success means money, fame, and fortune for Americans and others out there. Different people define success differently, but the growing popularity of financial success takes center stage and warrants some discussion on the matter. People pursue financial success for many reasons, but commonly we can see that this race is unending for reasons that will be explained later.

Now, we measure success by money. The amount of money we have defines our degree of success. It places us in a social class that we often remain in until our deaths.

Money defines the measure of a man.

I will not name this famed individual whose name is well known in pop culture. You may think a businessperson of his stature and unimaginable wealth may have something capitalistic up his sleeve. But surprisingly, I agree with the chap, too. After establishing and excelling with several startups, the man has something special to say that is laudable.

Material wealth has nothing to do with success. It is the reverse!

That is true indeed. So many people measure their success by the money parked in their accounts (even better with more accounts and more money). Another popular belief is the rich /affluent people you have in the circle that defines the measure of success.

I wager that money is no metric for success and satisfying life. As a matter of fact, I think happiness trumps everything else. I have sound reasoning for that but more on that later.

The famed entrepreneur began business with a different purpose. It was more about making a difference in people's lives and adding value to them, while less focus was on taking the forprofit company. It worked in his favor since the ideology was right, and as a result, he replicated this in his future ventures.

This famed entrepreneur had cracked the code. Happiness is the right metric to measure success, and it is the key to it.

If more money means more happiness is a recipe for disaster. You are tied to the system if this mindset prevails (Americans are stuck in this cycle).

The lesson turns out to be accurate time and again. Money helps to a certain point. When you are in a low-income bracket, money improves your overall well-being. After reaching a certain economic well-being point, you are no happier and more satisfied than a billionaire. This is the reality people need to understand and find hard to grasp. Americans work hard, hoping to be richer someday, and it will undoubtedly raise their contentment levels.

Secondly, the system is not supporting you either in your pursuance of the so-called material wealth. Look at the U.S. alone for now. It has a vast complex of multinational and transnational corporations. These corporations have grown and scale more than other corporations during the past five decades. However, the market value of the employees has declined rapidly during the same time while others have progressed. This shift toward decline is not due to the service-sector economy but rather the rules that disfavor the employees. The political system is rigged, too. Thanks to voter suppression, money in the system, and gerrymandering, the employees are disadvantaged, leading to economic inequality. As a result, rules are created to favor the rich, further fueling economic inequality.

For some people, the definition of success was clear to them. It revolved around collecting a massive pile of cash, being exceptional at your academics, and maybe leading the country in some shape or form. Anything else apart from this was a waste of time, signifying unimportant goals to accomplish.

Yes. You are one of those full-on believers because the old-school philosophy makes sense, and instances are all around living the life. You aim to follow the roadmap to riches by becoming a surgeon or some other white-collar designation at a renowned firm and hopefully become a millionaire on the eve of retirement or earlier, provided you play the cards right. You believe in working hard to earn the top dollar and leave a mark on others with your legacy. You are maybe a captain of the industry and attend several guest speaker sessions in universities and seminars. And weekends are for families and other excursions.

Life is good.

However, this is hardly an original idea. Many are hoping to see this day in some shape or form. The Americans are sold the American dream. Its allure is that much. A mass majority of U.S. citizens hope to be rich someday. And the youth is waiting for that day, buying into that dream just as their predecessors did.

Unfortunately, just five percent of Americans reach that point. Amazingly, those who get this dream are born into money. I am saying they inherit it. Around sixty percent of the U.S. wealth is inherited wealth. The billionaires you see in the latest issue of Forbes magazine were born into rich families. It is the easiest way and most common way to gain wealth.

However, this puts the working-class professionals at a disadvantage. So, the working-class professionals are in a tough spot and nowhere in the competition. More so, wealth begets wealth since the affluent are paid for owning their wealth. As a result, their wealth is forever. It will persist and spread over the course of generations. Unfortunately, the working class of the American population will never accumulate this much wealth till retirement. It means that the overall wealth retains among the wealthier lot of America. At the same time, those under the working-class bracket will continue to toil, followed by their children repeating the cycle.

Sudden Riches: Life is Set Now

Who does not think that an excellent six-figure salary will lead them to the life they want? Some people get lottery tickets, hoping their rotten luck would amount to something one fine morning. Maybe winning a massive pile of money will solve everything wrong in their lives. They can clear their credit card debt and mortgage payments and move into other material wants and wealth areas.

I will clear some misconceptions here, too.

The important thing is to spend in relation to your income. Now let us take an example here. Professional-level players in the NBA and NFL earn a cool sum of $1-4 million each year. But this sum quickly disappears, thanks to their reckless spending and bad financial choices along the way. As a matter of fact, they are broken soon after their public retirement. Nearly 80% of the lottery winners are bankrupt after two years and see severe financial stress. Five years later, they have royally fucked up their finances and are almost on the streets at this point.

The same issue is with the motherfucking lottery winners. These assholes are the worst of the worst. Any lottery winner splurges the money won, and it takes around a year before they are broken yet again. The issue is that money does not solve anything. It is the mindset that matters.

I am speaking from experience here.

I have a friend who later became a cautionary tale in my memory. We will call this schmuck Larry. Now, Larry won $16 million in the lottery back in 1990. The lottery amount is usually in installments. After a few weeks of receiving the first pot of cash, the blonde jackass spent around $3 million in senseless spending. He had airplanes, mansions, boats, and a fleet of cars. He did everything that someone would do when he got some extra money. That is just the typical mindset of most Americans.

In this case, his dream had come true. But the dye was cast. His condition was worse than before. He said that life was good before the lottery money came along. Thanks to his senseless spending, he was fucked in the ass. The guy died on a monthly disability check of $450 a month. His rags-to-riches story came crashing down in a matter of the same year. This is what happens when people with absolutely next to no financial literacy have money. They usually lack the prowess to manage their funds.

Despite earning $300 million throughout his career, professional boxer and heavyweight champion Mike Tyson filed for bankruptcy in 2003 with $30 million in debt. The fact that so many of our actions or motivations in life are driven by an underlying need or desire to gain money raises a fundamental issue about money itself. However, there appears to be little purpose in getting money if we can't seem to manage it. The following are some real accounts of people who either acquired or inherited large sums of money but lost them rapidly due to various careless or unrestrained behaviors.

Graham Roos received the $750,000 inheritance when he was just 26 years old following the passing of his great aunt. Even though he knew he would inherit something, the amount of it surprised him since it was more significant than he had ever imagined.

Roos assumed he was in a state of financial comfort when the money arrived in his bank account. He quit his job right once and went on a lavish spending binge. The money disappeared quickly, but he paid little attention to the shrinking balance. His spending mainly was on expensive vacations and works of art, but his partying and drug use would ultimately send him into a downward spiral. By the time he had used up the money in his bank account, he had racked up debt and needed to start working again to keep from going hungry.

Maureen O'Conner, a prominent person in her own right who was well-liked in politics, was competing for a seat on the San Diego City Council when she fell in love with and wed Robert O. Peterson. Peterson founded the fast-food chain Jack in the Box, and upon his passing, his widow received an inheritance of more than $50 million.

She developed a gambling addiction that primarily focused on video poker after receiving a brain tumor diagnosis and dealing with the pain associated with the deaths of her spouse and several of her close friends. Despite earning almost $1 billion in prizes in less than ten years through her self-described "grief gambling," she ended up with less than she had before. She was found guilty of money laundering for diverting funds from her husband's non-profit organization to pay off gambling bills, which only worsened her predicament. Despite receiving a postponed jail term, she was left penniless due to restitution and court fees.

Barbara Hutton, who earned the moniker "Poor Little Rich Girl," was the Woolworth fortune's heir. She received her inheritance of $50 million on her 21st birthday in the early 1930s, which, adjusted for inflation, would be over $900 million today - an incredible figure at any point in history. Her mother's passing by suicide in 1933 resulted in her receiving an inheritance.

Despite having a wealthy upbringing, the child Hutton developed into a severely insecure adult. Her mother battled depression, while her father was generally absent from her life. Shopping was Hutton's weakness, especially for her loved ones, whom she showered with pricey presents like jewelry, haute couture, and even works of art that had formerly belonged to Marie Antoinette. Her flaws weren't limited to her expenditures. Her wealth diminished over a string of seven spouses and countless relationships, leaving her with virtually nothing when she passed away in 1979 at age 66.

It's challenging to think of any actor with more than 35 years of acting experience who is a more excellent star than Johnny Depp. Depp established an artistic reputation in the early 1990s with classic movies like "Edward Scissor Hands" and "What's Eating Gilbert Grape." Still, he succeeded with his portrayal of the swaggering Captain Jack Sparrow in the "Pirates of the Caribbean" series.

Johnny Depp received an excellent $20 million compensation for each movie, but his films' box office success hasn't always matched their star power. In 2015 and 2016, Forbes called Depp, the Hollywood actor who earned the most money, too much.

Perhaps it's not surprising then that Depp's extravagant spending has resulted in financial difficulties, including spending $30,000 per month on wine and $3 million to fire the ashes of writer Hunter S. Thompson from a cannon.

Depp resolved a $25 million lawsuit in 2018 alleging financial mismanagement by his former management team.

John Hervey, a member of the English monarchy, received his inheritance when he turned 21 in the late 1970s. According to estimates, the $6 million endowments would equal nearly $65 million. Through a succession of wise investments in businesses like real estate, oil, and other ventures, this fortune was also enhanced during his 20s.

Hervey may have been a good investor, but he preferred to lead a lavish lifestyle that swiftly outpaced his substantial wealth. Yachts, sports vehicles, and escorts consumed much of his money, but these costs paled to the compulsive drug habit he had acquired. In ten years, more than $9 million of his money was lost to cocaine and heroin. His drug use led to several drug crimes, one of which led to deportation, and the costs started to rise. He was impoverished by the early 1990s and died shortly after from organ failure brought on by his drug usage.

Clint Murchison Jr., the oil tycoon's son, inherited $200 million upon his father's passing in the late 1960s. Today, the value of his inheritance would exceed $400 million. Murchison Jr. was raised to enjoy life's finer pleasures, and his use of his inheritance would be consistent with this.

Murchinson Jr. preferred to have fun with his wealth instead of making wise investments, in contrast to his father, who was a diligent investor. In 1960, he made his first significant investment, helping start the Dallas Cowboys football franchise. He spent millions not just on the football team but also on various other businesses, such as restaurants, oil, real estate, and even a radio station. He lost much money on his ventures, and the 1980s real estate and oil bubble burst left him deeply in debt. He was forced to file for bankruptcy at the age of 85, and two years later, after liquidating all of his assets, he passed away.

A Part of the Rat Race

Now, let us assess the fucked-up cycle of the working professionals. There is a reason the Americans are known for their lack of time. They are in a hurry to get things done, and I am unsure if the culture is likely to change anytime in the future without a mandate. The horizon of the U.S. shows no interest on that front. Amazingly, these people comprise a vast portion of the American populace. They are the engine of the American economy and are burning up generations to generations.

Their mindset works a certain way, and unfortunately, they cannot see the wood for the trees.

They get a job in a firm and look at the corporate ladder— that is their motherfucking gravy train.
Am I wrong here?

So, your income will typically increase annually/biannually as the income stream grows and the lifestyle betters. The company gives a bloody raise which compels you to celebrate and go all in. You splurge on clothing, fine wine, and all the good things in life. These luxury items are pricey and even pricier to store and maintain.

But who the fuck is complaining?

Life is good, and you are a happy camper. This lifestyle takes a life of its own and works harder and longer hours to earn more. You are waiting for the next raise at the office to push the envelope a little more—another year and a little more. Upon completion, you are pining for a benchmark that will be your peak of financial freedom. And the journey is complete.

They have reached Maslow's Hierarchy of Needs.

However, when you have reached that point eventually in your life, another startling realization dawns. This was breaking the ceiling. In all your biased, limited, and filtered wisdom, you simply repeat this process by spending more and earning more. The cycle continues until you finally decide to hang your boots.

Congratulations! The system has gamed you.

It was rigged, to begin with!

There is a phrase for it, and I like it a lot. Psychologists call the hedonic cycle treadmill a nerdy phrase for the rat race. When people step on this hedonic treadmill, their mindset is similar. A little more money will get them to their desired lifestyle and material wants. Their needs and wants are on this bloody upward trajectory that keeps raising the bar and moving the needle. Since they are constantly on this unending treadmill, the nagging thought is money—just a little more until they have reached a point of satisfaction.

Most Americans are chasing this phantom goal of financial freedom in a system that is rigged to lose.

We have learned nothing from history either. The median income of an American household in 1967 was nearly $40,000.
One in twenty-five people had cable, and one-fifth had color T.V.s in their homes. Today, we have come a long way since then. It is the internet age, and everyone owns car and other consumer electronics.

Life is good, right? We have reached the height of human civilization. But the happiness index is still nearly the same as the people living in the 1960s—there is more money and even more comfortable life than before. But we have not moved the needle in terms of happiness.
What gives?

This brings me back to the original point—you are chasing happiness—you are not chasing riches and wealth. The mass media has the average American convinced that wealth equals happiness. And that is such a myth and wildly inaccurate. I agree that money is essential to achieve the goals in your mind and pay off that mortgage, preserve the future, and ensure an enjoyable life. And from all this discussion, I can tell you that buying stuff left, right, and center does not mean satisfaction.

Are you an expert on personal finance and financial freedom? It is a rhetorical question. I know that few Americans know the premise of what I am talking about and the work it requires to get there. But more on that later. Most Americans are tied to their day job and chained by the system. Imagine if we broke free, the system might collapse. Thanks to the mindless zombies, the great American economy is up and running. Although it was that simple, I would not be here, and neither would you. You would not be making stupid financial decisions and running into debt all the time. Many things play into this. But I would first start it from the beginning and take it from there.

What Does it Lead to Eventually?

I think that Americans, for the most part, are fulfilling some parameters of Maslow's Hierarchy of Needs model. This model has five steps of basic human needs. The last stage is that of perfection and control of the other domains. Abraham Maslow organized the pyramid into a five-tier model:

• **Physiological needs:** This is the most basic stage of human needs, involving primary needs like shelter, water, and food.

• **Safety needs:** The next stage involves financial and security needs, comprising money, peace, and urban security.

- **Love and belonging needs:** The last lower-level needs involve personal interaction and relationships. It includes family and friend bonds and other relationships.
- **Esteem needs:** This is a form of higher need and involves respect in several domains. It can involve esteem after assessing oneself while earning the respect of others, too.
- **Self-actualization needs:** The person has acquired the idealized form as a person. It is the highest position on the pyramid.

So, you might see the rat race is centered over the initial three areas of need in the model. The Americans are invested in physiological, safety, and love needs for the most part. Their self-actualization needs remain unfulfilled and leave room for much improvement.

They should be chasing self-actualization. Being wealthy does not guarantee happiness. You and I will see the most affluent people with fame and fortune committing suicide and victims of anxiety and loneliness. On the flip side of the coin, impoverished children laugh their hearts out, seemingly enjoying life to the fullest despite having nothing.

I will end the chapter with this: true happiness is not the pursuit of money/material wealth. It is existing outside the circumstances and feeling satisfied with it. This is what self-actualization will help accomplish.

Chapter 2
Corporate Slaves

'Get a job that you have always wanted' is dated advice. Confucius was the first man who spoke the iconic words: Do what you love. He meant something along the lines of finding a line of work that we love and taking it on for our lives, allowing it to consume us. This famed advice has been reiterated countless times throughout history. Warren Buffet and Maya Angelou also echoed these thoughts, proposing to opt for things people love to do. The earlier works of notable thought leaders proclaim doing what you love, which, in layman's words, means opting for a career you love. This has been a 'done-to-death discussion area, and I have no intention of harping about it.

Interestingly, we should also look at the opposite side of the picture. What about those people who do not enjoy what they do? What about them? Fortunately, Steve Jobs suggests doing great work by loving what you do.

But research work in the area stands opposed. Contemporary research is now going against this conventional wisdom. More and more people are finding themselves dissatisfied at work. Adding on to their misery, they are disgruntled, disengaged, and feel uncertain about their futures. The pandemic has exaggerated these fears since it jumpstarted a downsizing spree as firms booted employees left, right and center.

For employees, no news is good news.

You wake up and find your measly existence trapped in a monotonous cycle every day. It is more of the same each day. You will wake up, have breakfast, leave for work, toil for nine hours and return home to your empty life.

This lifestyle is dull, dreary, and rather lethal, which becomes clear later in the chapter.

The capitalistic society changes the parameters of success. Previously, it was human values and compassion that defined people. Capitalism changes the ballgame altogether. People now gauge their self-esteem based on their buying power and social status. It has become the new normal in this day and age, So the bigger the check, the better the prospects of upscaling your god-damn lifestyle. The vicious cycle compels people to stay inside the loop, preventing them from deviating from their capitalistic-ordained path even if they wanted.

At the end of it, they pay a higher price by being part of the system that burns them and throws them out when they become unviable to the bigger machinery.

It is a compulsive rut, and there is no escaping it either, as long as you are a corporate slave.

Amazingly (and unfortunately), I discovered a few striking similarities between a corporate slave and the ones that landed on U.S. soil ages ago:
So, let us contrast the two.

The African Slave

- He is an individual who is the legal property of someone else and is subsequently obligated to abide by the rules.
- He is a person who works quite hard, but the remuneration and appreciation are always underwhelming.
- He, as an individual, depends heavily on his owner and is controlled by an iron fist.
- He is easily replaceable by another slave.

I know you are connecting the dots by now, but there is more to come.

So, now, let us examine the corporate culture at large:

- In a corporate culture, the employee forcibly follows orders. He must complete something under the time allotted and set quality standards. Anything besides this brings the competency of an employee into question. The senior management will decide about the asset or liability of an employee.
- The monetary compensation might be good, but where is the appreciation? Are the performing employees appreciated or the ones who excel at flattery? Slaving away may sometimes be less fruitful than sucking up to the boss you cannot stand to see otherwise.
- The employees go out of their way to stay in good books. It is because their future depends on goodwill. As a result,

the said employee will sideline personal/professional issues to climb the corporate ladder.

• The day-by-day tasks and activities are completed under the control of the company owner. As a matter of fact, these activities can be shuffled in order of their priority as the boss demands.

• The employee must follow the organizational directives regardless of how senseless they can get.

Sounds familiar?

America is built on lies atop more lies. People are feeding into these lies, thinking they are true. However, they are far from accurate.

I will explain my point below.

The Emancipation Proclamation was Abraham Lincoln's famous speech that freed the slaves. In one way, it was just empty words because the American system did not change much. The premise of the speech was something along these lines:

• Free the working slaves
• Provide them with rights and citizenship
• Form a great society

All of this sounds familiar, right?

As a matter of fact, the slavery system was not abolished at all. It was expanded to include people of all colors, castes, and creeds to guarantee a thriving slave market that was far more versatile and cheaper for the sleazy owners.

You may have heard the term thrown around 'The American Dream.' Yes, that old chestnut. It is the biggest scam/con America has played in the world. Even today, people arrive on U.S. soil to pursue their 'American Dream.'

It is based on the premise that when you work 'hard enough' and suck up to the American system, you will eventually earn the keys to the kingdom. It involves the same old nonsense when you get a raise at work or some much-needed promotion; you are well on your way there.

This dream works on the carrot-and-stick model—it is simply an imaginary incentive that keeps the American people busy and working hard for the profit of the far and few elitists of the nation.

Nothing has changed if you see things in hindsight. This slavery system has now transitioned into a full-on race struggle involving different social classes vying against the one-percent elite. But it is fighting for a losing cause. The standard model is that you are in a typified 9-5 situation. The wages pay off for the food on the table and ensuring the roof stays over your head. Either you earn the check or die from poverty. Otherwise, you cannot feed yourself or thrive in this system, which means you are at your most vulnerable in this arrangement. As a result, you can never be a free man when you depend on someone for survival.

You will always remain a slave.

Furthermore, if you work your ass off daily just because you can spend this money for basic life amenities, then these labor efforts are an end to means for self-preservation. In this system, you cannot attain social mobility.

This, by definition, is slavery, and you are still no different than those slaves from a few centuries ago.

But that is not all. When we account for inflation, the average wages of a slave were higher than the salary of today's minimum wage worker.

Essentially, slaves were worth more than the average modern-day minimum wage employees of this day and age. And I am only scratching the surface here. These slaves from a few centuries ago were worth more, and they had it much better than your lot!

I do not deny the disgusting, demoralizing, and corrupt nature of slavery as a concept. Still, the prior slavery system was relatively better in contrast to the slavery system of modern times.

The slaves of before were required to be in good health back in the day. The slave owners could not afford a diseased or weakish slave. After all, they had to work the fields all day long. A diseased worker meant less output for the day. Resultantly, the slaveowners paid for the doctor visits as well as the healthcare bills. So, amazingly, the slaves had free-of-cost healthcare in those days.

On the other hand, we have ill-fated cases where people cannot afford healthcare. A lady would be bleeding on the subway but screaming she cannot afford American healthcare. People with epilepsy carry notes that dictate people not to call an ambulance. And then, cases of children dying of illnesses are common since their parents cannot afford medical bills, thanks to this imbalanced system.

The present corporate slavery is something of a disposable commodity for the owners and 'forces that be.' In the previous era, slaves were well-treated, well-fed, and well-rested since they worked the fields, and that required an extra level of fitness. These people were given accommodation as well, sometimes with the owners for proper care and look after. They were taken care of well, all things considered.

We are not as lucky, having to manage our accommodation, food, and utility expenses. Everything comes out of the measly paycheck, which is a struggle for modern-day Americans. Many Americans live in debt, struggling to make ends meet, thanks to corporate slavery.

The point is that corporate slavery freely exists masquerading as the free market system. In this system, the livability of the employees depends on their paycheck. The labor exploitation is clear and quite apparent here. As long as you are a part of the corporate slavery system, you will have unequal bargaining power and remain at the receiving end. As an employee, you are forced to perform throughout the year and under tight deadlines. Any hint of incompetence or negligent behaviors makes you a marked man for termination. Any burnout and effects on physical and mental well-being resulting from living and breathing in this system can lead to detrimental impacts. In his fiction novel "The Circle," author Dave Eggers (2013) explains what it's like to work for a digital giant. Mae Holland, a woman in her 20s, is the subject of this story. She manages to secure a job at The Circle, a technology social media company. The Three Wise Men-led The Circle, which employs "hundreds of outstanding young minds" each week, has earned the prize for "most admired business" four times in a row. After accepting the post, the young woman happily takes her belongings and leaves for her new home in the corporate world.

She strongly desires to advance professionally in the organization since it promises to provide her with a fulfilling career as long as she remains committed and involved. As the events of the story unfold, the protagonist finds that she is becoming addicted to her line of work. Why wouldn't she? The company provided her with more perks than she could handle, including free gym membership, access to the company cafeteria, the newest technology, and free accommodation "on campus" (rather than in offices). The firm said these rewards were offered to show how much it valued its "talented" employees. One of the intriguing products of the "Circle" is "TruYou," a single integrated user interface that handles and streamlines every internet contact and transaction. Thanks to the data uploaded throughout a customer's interactions with the company, "TruYou" practically owns the entire life of every user of the interface. Yes, this does sound familiar.

As the story progresses through several chapters, our young professional character in the book soon reaches her career's apex while employed by the business. She is allowed to report directly to the board, known as "The Three Wise Men," and is always available. After each month, she also ensures that her staff has accomplished those objectives. Many people nowadays probably find themselves in similar situations. There is no longer time for off-topic conversation. Your family begins to believe you are boring since your phone pings every two minutes, emails keep coming in, and your inbox is packed with territorial disputes for which you were never required to be in writing. Your kids no longer bother bringing you their schoolwork since you are using your right eye to check your emails and your left eye to look at their painting simultaneously. They no longer come because they perceive your lack of interest in them. Just as in "The Circle," we start pulling away from the people who matter the most.

We bring two phones to a restaurant (a personal one and a work one). We never consider leaving them behind. Many people claim that they do it in case anything occurs at work. To ensure everything is OK back at the office, we continue browsing between the entrée and the main dish on our phones. Many individuals are unaware that their business depends on more than one person to conduct its operations. But occasionally, a lot of us think we're indispensable. In all honesty, we are not.

On vacation, we bring two phones and a laptop in case the boss wants a presentation or an urgent report that was not finished in time before we left. So much for our baggage weight and lengthier lines at airport security to scan all of our workplace equipment. The corporate phone is turned off after we arrive at our location and check into our hotel. You've got a crucial phone call to make. You spend two hours on the phone, and a voice asks if you have any comments at the end. You didn't have any and realized you didn't need to be there.

Meetings and conference calls take up virtually all of our weekly schedule and last for 16 hours every day. The task we couldn't complete throughout the previous week was subsequently completed during the weekend. Some of us organized "fictitious meetings," which we later exploited to get some of our backlog done and block their calendar. At first, it runs smoothly, but we start double booking soon after. The result turns out to be chaos.

Returning to our narrative's climax, our young professional returns to the beginning, where it all began (I won't spill the beans and ruin it for you if you want to read it). She learns that we don't necessarily need to be connected all the time and that being a "Slave to the Corporate World" is not a life worth living.

So, welcome to modern-styled slavery, which we call corporate slavery. It is cutthroat, brutal, and has you sweating it out all day long at a fraction of what the owner is taking home each day.

So, here is a question: Ever thought about escaping the plantation?

Why should an individual keep toil away at his desk job? Why does he prefer the vicious trap of corporate slavery every day?

Well, the answer to that is easy.

People measure their self-esteem based on their social status and their buying power. Self-actualization stands for something very different from what it is disguised as and then sold off to anyone who wishes to survive in this day and age. In the free market parlance, self-actualization means enjoying a hefty paycheck and funding the lifestyle one wishes to live and maintain. In doing so, the place in society is maintained, and selfesteem is secured. Holding a corporate job is held in high regard.

However, there is a downside to all of this. It is an artificial sense of gratification. The false sense of security prevents us from connecting with our inner self. As a result, the individual compromises their freedom. It is too late when the delusion clears, paving the way for reality to sink in. One is tied to the system and at the receiving end by that time.

You cannot have financial freedom in such a system. The law is not on your side since it has sided up with the employer here.

Freedom of Speech in a Workplace

As an American, I am born and bred with the right to speak my mind. Our First Amendment promises everyone freedom of speech which is a part of the Bill of Rights.

So, freedom of speech means different things to different people.

You can abuse the hell out of your annoying dad, pesky sister, or slacker brother. It is fair game, man. Freedom of speech also extends to the bloody internet, where you give someone detestable a piece of your mind.

P.S. That has changed a bit with all those hate speech rules and stuff to limit personal attacks and foul language, which has toned down the digital space quite well. But still, you can speak your mind there. The internet allows your thoughts to flow freely. So, if you dislike an opinion, you can criticize the person saying anything under the sun. Maybe that person is a whiny right-winger or advocating typewriter maintenance—you let loose on the abuse without thinking twice. You have the freedom to speak at your disposal.

This freedom of speech also extends to other offline places.

For instance, do you dislike the food at the restaurant? No problem. Start abusing the head chef or the management for poor service. You have nothing to lose here. Companies in the service industries are wary of criticism because bad word travels like wildfire. They will probably go out of their way to treat you like a king or something.

Now, guess where your freedom of speech rights vanishes into thin air? You guessed it—the workplace!

I take issue with the constitution here because it remains silent on freedom of speech at work. For the employees, they practically do not exist since the policies and laws favor the employer here.

Talk about one-sided rights!

In a workplace setting, your freedom of speech rights is limited. And as a matter of fact, your employer is well within your rights to pursue legal action against you for something you said in person or wrote on the email/chatting software.

Let me explain how limited your rights are once you step into that office the next time.

The First Amendment in the American constitution protects the citizens with some limitations. The American Congress cannot enact a law that prevents/hinders the right of an individual to say something and how they say it. The federal and state governments have added it, but it is still not absolute. As a matter of fact, the law protects citizens from government actions, not from companies of any size.

So, for instance, a police officer cannot arrest you on the road or the sidewalk for donning a Democrats baseball cap. He has no legal standing for doing so. However, once you step inside the office wearing a Democrats cap, your employer is well within your rights to lay you off. And you have no legal standing in a court of law either when you cross that bridge.

So, think twice the next time you almost say a foul word to your line manager or department head. Your seat at the firm depends on how nicely you behave with the senior management who want a workforce that performs as to the set standards, takes their paycheck, and leaves without irking them. So, clearly, you are not the one winning in this system.

But all is not lost. There is a way to win and win big in this system.
Let me explain a scenario here:

So, imagine if you had enough money in the account. You are sitting peacefully at your desk when a boss who had a bad day comes up and starts screaming about the quarterly report. The remainder of the department sneaks from their small cubicles to see the commotion. Your crush is also interested by this point.

You are sweating looking at the scene created by this fucking schmuck. But suddenly, you stand up to him and look him in the eye. The boss looks at you directly, and his face becomes livid. He tells you to sit down, which you do, but grab him by his balls.

Some gasps and cries are heard in the background, but you look at him defiantly in the eye, clutching them tighter.

"Let it go, moron," he says weakly.

You let go and calmly say, "I quit."

There is muted silence in the hallway while everyone waits with bated breath.

Turning away, you do not pack and take the elevator to the ground floor instead.

"I have 'fuck you' money," you loudly announce, leaving the building forever and the colleagues confused.

The rest of the staff scratches their heads while your crush Googles the term and finds out. She gasps!

That is what I am talking about. You should have 'fuck you' money.

When you have earned financial freedom, you can talk shit about the boss' mom to him without thinking twice of the consequences. With "fuck you" money, you can do anything and everything.

The concept of 'fuck you' revolves around the premise that you have enough money to stand up and leave the firm the same day. You no longer need the firm's payroll. It is too small and paltry to satisfy your growing needs. With 'fuck you money,' you have reached the stage of self-actualization where the world runs to your tune. You are the Pied Piper leading others behind you.

We can easily say, 'Fuck you, Trump," or 'Biden is a hillbilly' from the comfort of social media and drawing-room discussions. But you cannot say something like this to your senior management and especially not until you are dependent on them.

******

The purpose of writing this chapter was to get a few things into your head. You need to fucking understand that America is not a free country, and you are not its free citizen. American freedom is an illusion, and a bad one at that.

There is no financial freedom in America unless you quit the system and see it from above—the system is rigged against you. Yeah, the odds are not stacked in your favor. As a matter of fact, America is like a casino that has a system in its place, preventing the people from big winnings. The people can only lose and lose big time. Coming out, they do not realize what happened to them.

America thrives on this system: The rich are taking advantage of the poor and will continue to rip them off until they realize it. So, the way I see it, you have two routes:

1. Prepare for a booty call with the rich
2. Become financially independent and leave the rat race

So, the next time your boss says, "Go fuck yourself, William," you should be prepared to cut him off and say, "Fuck you, Harry, you are the lowest form of life. I do not need your money. Shove it up where the sun does not shine."

You will be a living legend within the walls of your firm. This is the main reason why we need to save money. Conventional preaching is money made to spend; if money is not used on buying goods and services, what is money for? As you can see from this chapter, freedom is the most valuable or priceless good and service. When we save enough money, we obtain so-called "fuck you" money, so we use these savings to buy freedom and the power to say no to things that are against our free will. When we take economics class, we are taught that money is used to buy goods and services; here, we need to add one more element- free will or freedom. Therefore, money can purchase goods, services, and freedom. When you spend money, you use the money to buy goods and services; when you save and invest money, you are using money to buy freedom. So, whether you spend the money or save and invest the money, you are constantly spending money; the only difference is what items you get. For centuries, people worldwide came to this country to seek the most valuable things they couldn't obtain from the Old World-freedom. That shows how much this country values freedom more than anything else. Shouldn't we use our hard-earned money to buy more valuable things? Yes, there are many expensive and luxury goods and services we can buy, but no matter how expensive they are, they all have prices. However, freedom is priceless. It is more valuable or luxurious than any other luxury items, such as a big mansion, fancy cars, expensive watches, a yacht, etc. Or let me put it this way: we need to save and adequately invest money because we need to buy ourselves out of this modern slavery. And how do we properly invest our hard-earned money to ensure we are not ripped off by this rigged system again? I will discuss it in chapters 7, 8, and 9.

Chapter 3
Give Me Liberty or Give Me Death!

They say what goes around comes around.

The point of this single line will become clear as we continue further below.

How did we lose our independence and sovereignty, and at what cost? Did we do things differently than our colonizers (the British Empire)? We were supposed to stand for something the European colonizers were not!

Let us see if we did that or not!

We, as a nation, won our independence after giving the British Empire a run for their motherfucking money (pun intended) with continuous wars and several of them under a ten-year period. The vast empire spread over several continents in the east and west was only a sum of its parts. The more its colonies rebelled, the weaker it would become since it was a primarily indirect rule, thriving from siphoning the resources of its colonies. Under George Washington, the British Empire faced stiff resistance several times, and with strategic advances, things fared badly for the colonizers.

Once the British Empire left us, we were still embroiled in slavery, which promulgated the Civil War of 1861-65 when the Confederate States decided to separate themselves from mainstream America. The ideological war was fought for a few years before the weakish rebellion was quashed. This was possible due to the military might of America as a whole.

We then fought against the oppression against civil rights that took quite some time to accomplish with its own share of bloodshed and violence. However, there was no capitalistic element tied to it.

Everything eventually resolved with time. The matter of colonies, the illegal land acquisitions and expansion of territories, and the rights of second-class citizens was resolved.

However, during this journey of becoming a nation, we still could not eliminate our biggest enemy. This enemy continues to oppress us each day and generations over time. Capitalism!

Indeed! Capitalism remains the sole oppressor. The American population is thrown into the rat race as soon as they are born. The throes of capitalism bind them in chains. The cycle keeps repeating itself, with new entrants ready through the system itself.

We intensely fought the British Empire to seek freedom from their financial enterprise and gain political freedom since it became clear that the U.S. colonies had no representation back in the U.K. Well, to no one's surprise, neither did the other colonies. It was supporting its own self-interests.

The rising discontent became a precursor for a revolution. However, I will show how this so-called revolution is nothing but a joke on the American people and the system it was fighting.

The Boston Tea Party

Our independence also started with capitalism tied in between. It all started on a wintery December night in 1773. Around a hundred men stormed the trading ships owned by the British Empire in Boston and tossed valuable tea cargo into the sea.

The disposal of the tea was a declaration of war against the British Empire. The people had realized the designs of their colonizers. They put themselves first before their subjects.

The sudden, unannounced rebellion became known as the infamous Boston Tea Party. It was a protest against taxes imposed by an indirect British government. The British government favored its East India Company, allowing lower taxes to perform its operations. Incidentally, it drove the local tea suppliers out of business since they could not compete with a giant and an advantage.

The British East India Company was today's version of a chain store that mass supplied tea (among other commodities) back to England. They understood the British government's monopolization, which disadvantaged its people, who had thought of themselves as loyalists. After all, they were still Englishmen on U.S. soil. The monopolization was oppressive and showed the capitalistic intentions of the British Empire.

Side note: Remember this point! It will come into use later on. Sometimes, we become the enemy we are fighting.

The colonial subjects loved their tea. It was tasty, cool, and sexy with a fragrance unlike any other. The caffeine hit struck a chord with the masses, becoming part and parcel of the colonial social structure, with the nobility and masses enjoying it just the same.

The issue of taxation was a tipping point for the people on U.S. soil.

Cue the American Capitalism

After continuous warring with the British Empire, the thirteen colonies of America gained independence in 1776. This independence came after around 170 years of the British Empire's rule. Even after the nation gained independence, its early years began showing faces of capitalism with only a population of 2.5 million people. So, even back then (and now), capitalism served despicable ends, noble aims, and a composite of the two.

During the nation's early years, slavery was a formula for amassing endless wealth. When the Civil War ended in 1865, the valley of Mississippi was surprisingly home to dozens of millionaires/per capita than the rest of the United States. The harvested cotton home-grown was the biggest export commodity of the newly formed nation. The hard-working African Americans still worked upon the plantation brought illegally from the African continent. The net worth of these enslaved individuals was more than all the factories and railroads in the nation. New Orleans had a banking capital that overshadowed New York City back in the day. Thanks to the suitable soil and climate for its growth, the nation was thriving on its cotton exports. People were getting richer and richer each year. We Americans had no hesitation in resorting to violence against the nonwhite populace. In pursuance of wealth, the white man continued his heavy-handed approach to labor and land.

We Americans chose barbarism, devious means to pursue poverty, cruelty and lawlessness, and totalitarianism to amass its wealth. There was no niceness in all of this.

So, as we look at the nation's history, it has been market oriented and capitalistic from the start. The settling of this nation was couched in capitalism when the transatlantic slave trade was kickstarted by the British Empire in its new colony spreading to different parts of America.

Even today, more and more Americans have amassed fortunes from the appreciation/depreciation of real estate values than other sources. But the land is just one piece of this epochal tale of American capitalism. From the start, Americans have shown a great willingness to pursue market forces with next-to-no hesitation.

During the early years of its inception, the Americans' appetite was a function of European deprivation in this new world of opportunity. The pent-up demand from the centuries came to the forefront. Initial America was pretty small and half the size of its present-day. There was plentiful land everywhere to capture post-independence and quite less resistance in comparison. These so-called Americans were hungry for land, pushing the natives out of their lands with amendments and stuff while capturing other areas with sheer force. America was getting bigger and bigger. The ambitions of the white man were just getting warmed up.

With land acquisitions, they continued to establish farms and ranches for themselves. Wealth was there to be taken with so much irrigable land to use.

This was the primitive form of the American Dream, far removed from industrialization.

The post-colonial period was just the beginning of the capitalism rush for the affluent. Everything was up for grabs— either via amendments or at gunpoint. Vast portions of land were either sold or given away generously by the government at throwaway prices. In their drive to acquire more and more land, the reps of the newly independent nation did not hesitate to dispossess one another or the Red Indians living there for thousands of years. At times, downright murder was sanctioned for land grabs. The details of this capitalistic drive are not very hunky-dory, as claims of theft/stolen property are still commonplace in some parts of America.

Since the land was available in abundance in their vast country, it became a key factor of production. The other elements involve capital, labor, and entrepreneurship to harness its full potential. At the nation's birth, capitalism fused these elements into a full-on operational system for pushing forward economic industry.

So, are you with me so far? Does this sound familiar and somewhat like the British Empire? How were the Americans of the newly formed land different than their predecessors? They were supposed to stand for something!

The seeds of this capitalism were sowed long ago. The Americans were doing what the British Empire did previously. Now, let us examine some of it. If I begin discussing the history here, it will take a few books before I am.

And I am not here for that. Aside from the oppressed enslaved people, entrepreneurs, and free yeoman farmers, a mass majority of the white population came on American soil as servants. Before the famed American Revolution, these individuals entered America from England, Ireland, Germany, and Scotland. The trips were voluntary and forced as well.

So, we can say that capitalism initially came in the first ships that landed on American soil. It took on different shapes and forms, all done in capitalism's good name, whether legal commerce, labor exchange to arrive in America, covering for religious freedom, or the slave trade.

Thus, the American heritage shows capitalism in its fabric much before its inception.

The Age of Industrialism

A new wave of industrialization replaced the phase of the agrarian economy. As a result, the American economy shifted from an agrarian to an industrial economy.

The American nation has millions of privately-owned companies today. Surprisingly, only far few existed when the nation was birthed in 1776. The trend of corporations was started by England, expanding its colonies across the board in America. In 1607, settlers arrived at Jamestown. It was called Virginia Company of London. Later, the Puritans founded Boston city in 1630 and worked under another British-owned company known as the Massachusetts Bay Company.

The owners of the Virginia Company had a considerable interest vested in tobacco production and its revenues. These Puritans were unmistakably capitalist in their intentions, and their actions, later on, demonstrate that as well. Their ideals were no different than the rest of the colonizers arriving on U.S. soil.

William Penn and his happy friends sought refuge in the new land. These folks were persecuted back in England for their religious beliefs. After acquiring a land grant in 1681, they began a new colony for religious and capitalist ends. Traders in Pennsylvania were becoming rich, international traders. Like the New England puritan merchants, they formed a network of relationships over continents.

Oh, another English firm played a decisive role in populating the land of America. This was the Royal African

Company chartered in 1672 and took over a major portion of the slave trade at the time. For maximum profiteering, this firm brought thousands of Africans against their will to the shores of America. Later on, it became a thriving trade, with thousands of seamen and white merchants taking an active part in this trade. The white merchants were on both sides of the Atlantic Ocean. Around ten million Africans were brought to the new land for hard labor. The destination mainly was Brazil or the Caribbean islands that served as fertile grounds for sugar farming.

History Repeating Itself

The country that was, among other reasons fighting monopoly soon found itself repeating the acts of its colonizer.

As it seems to me, America is founded on a bed of lies. These lies continue to this day. And the famous American Dream is much as a fraud as it was back in the day. It is the same as everything that its predecessor did before the nation gained independence.

I can show several instances where American privately owned corporations pulled up 'East India Company' on its people when industrialization took hold.

Monopolies first entered the U.S. with the colonial administration. These large-scale public works were set to make life more hospitable for the European settlers. However, these companies became too big to fail, as I will show.

As of today, the three most infamous U.S. monopolies rattled the country to the core. They dictated the terms of operation and engagement for decades on end. These companies are:

- U.S. Steel (owned by Andrew Carnegie)
- Standard Oil Company (owned by John D. Rockefeller)
- American Tobacco Company

These monopolies hail back to the era of British colonizers who awarded major companies' exclusive contracts to shape up the new world. This kickstarted a reign of these corporations from the 19th to 20th century, who maintained control over their respective commodities, disallowing any competition and smaller business units to enter their so-called coveted space. While having a capitalistic intent, they defied the norms of free market capitalism. As a result, they openly monopolized their markets (tobacco, steel, and oil), driving high prices and eliminating their competition.

Sherman's Hammer

Since the monopolies abovementioned had established a system that favored themselves, it created a furor and resentment among the common populace. But aside from the workers in these companies, small business owners took the hit just the same because the policies of the larger businesses made it very difficult to fight on a level playing field.

In response to public outcry regarding the price-fixing abuses, thanks to the monopolies, the U.S. government was forced to pass the Sherman Antitrust Act in 1890. The act immediately barred monopolistic practices and trusts, often unreasonable sanctions on international and interstate trade. The act allowed the government to break monopolies into several smaller pieces, easing the competition and allowing an equal playing field.

But still, this did little over the next five decades, which saw the emergence of domestic monopolies. The antitrust legislation took on big players, breaking them up into smaller units later. In doing so, it had varying levels of success to this end. The act was keen on looking at good and bad monopolies from a public perspective.

One case is the International Harvester which developed cost-effective agricultural equipment for the predominantly agrarian economy of America. This company was untouchable. Then there is the case of American Tobacco, which was long suspected of overcharging for the price of cigarettes. At that point in time, cigarettes were touted to cure several ailments (menstrual cramps, and asthma, among others). However, in 1911, it was broken into several smaller units.

Therefore, monopolies are bad. They go against the principles of a free-market economy. It is what the British Empire was doing when it was selling tea, eliminating the competition in its attempt to become the only supplier standing in the market.

When a company has exclusive production controls in a particular industry, it becomes a monopoly. This is impossible under a free-market system because free-market economies allow equal competition and a level playing field for all the competitors. When the competition is entitled to free flow, no single supplier/seller can gain exclusive control over a particular industry.

This brings us to an oligopoly, an industry with little to no competition. Even in a free market, it is not easy to establish a massive company due to the investment required. This is how Andrew Carnegie was able to establish himself as an oligopoly. Now take the case of Andrew Carnegie here.

He created a monopoly of an unmatched scale. His corporation was later sold off to J.P. Morgan, which thus became U.S. Steel. The company was paralleling the size of Standard Oil. However, it also did very little innovation despite its enormous resources. Other smaller companies were more innovative in their limited resources. While U.S. Steel had a whopping market share of 60% in steel production, the rival firms were hungrier and more efficient than the steel giant. As a result, U.S. Steel stagnated when it came to innovation. The smaller entities took on the giant silently, chipping away its market share over time.

Capitalism is not a religion, but it is considered above religion. It is bound to happen in America or other places that hold capitalism in reverence. However, we should know that capitalism is no savior. It is the devourer of systems, chewing out those unfit to adjust to its design.

The despicable system has succeeded over the years while socialism and communism rose to the surface as prominent systems. However, as we all know very well, these two systems could not be applied globally, nor do their systems guarantee the happiness of their subjects entirely.

But one thing is for sure. No system is perfect. Communism has its issues, while socialism provides an extra blanket relief, whereas capitalism surpasses all of them with a free market system, allowing everyone to reach their potential of success.

But we should know that a working system does not mean it is also booming. Capitalism paves the way for monopolies to form, which only government policies can counteract. This becomes increasingly difficult in countries at their knees financially and is vulnerable to capitalistic monopolies created by large corporations. You can find several instances of this happening all over the globe where major companies (transnational companies) dictate terms of operation to the government. Withdrawing from their countries can spell disaster for smaller countries than these corporations.

So, over time, we have tried to replace the capitalistic system with communism and socialism. However, none of them worked to the effectiveness of capitalism.

We also know that the government and national-level politics do not facilitate systems that work against capitalism.

Therefore, it is more a matter of helping yourself leave the system.

Do you want financial freedom?

Then quit the rat race right now. But if right away is not an option (for many people), then start developing systems to help you leave the rat race. Otherwise, you are stuck in the system like a lab rat.

The change will begin individually since the political machinery and the governmental systems will not support you on this journey.

You are very much alone.

The 'powers that be' do not wish that you defect from the system. Their well-being lies in your involvement in the system. Otherwise, it will fall on its knees.

Now, as you can see, any government's primary goal is to enhance the wealth of nations, not the wellness of nations. Therefore, we ought to find ways to improve and ensure our wellness at the individual level. We may see some helpful solutions from the philosophy of Stoicism. (We will discuss more of this in chapter 10) The core teaching of Stoicism is to divide this world into external and internal worlds. The external world is mainly things out of our control, while the internal world is things we have complete or more control over. People have discovered the flaws of capitalism since the 19th century.

Hence, they attempted to seek alternative solutions from the external world, such as using socialism and communism in the hope of replacing capitalism. However, the reality has proven that communism and socialism have even more deficiencies than capitalism. Thus, to reach financial or real freedom, we have two alternatives: 1, seek solutions from the internal world; 2, use the bright side of capitalism to serve our cause.

As mentioned, several times in this and previous chapters, saving and adequately investing money is critical for seeking real and financial freedom. Adopting a minimalist and simpler lifestyle, finding a higher level of life pursuit, and focusing more on our inner happiness are all measures we can take to seek solutions from our internal world, which we can have more control over. We will discuss these topics more in chapters 4, 5, and 6. On the other hand, we can utilize the bright side of capitalism to let money work for us, in other words, to enslave money instead of being enslaved by money. There are two primary components of the capitalist system: capital vs. labor. People who have capital are the oppressor in this system. People who only have labor are the oppressed in this system. This brings us back to the importance of saving money. The more money you save, the more capital you have, and the more you can benefit from this system.

On the other hand, the more money you waste on unnecessary items, the less capital you have, and the more this system can oppress you. America has the best and most sophisticated financial system in the world. Not only does it help to fuel the growth of prominent corporations, but it also provides opportunities for ordinary people to be shareholders and stakeholders of this system. But the premise is that you need to have capital. Those mega-cap high-tech companies, such as Microsoft, Google, Amazon, Apple, and Facebook, have become increasingly monopolistic and dominant in the global economy. Smaller businesses and competitors find it harder to compete with these giants. Since we cannot defeat this system, our other choice is to at least participate in this system to a certain extent. No matter how big the universe is, it is made up of tiny atoms. Same as investing our money. We don't need a lump sum of money to reach financial freedom. By adopting a good habit of investing a little bit of money each month into the capitalist system via the capital market, we can let the magical, the eighth wonder of the world, power of compounding brings us excellent results over time. Unfortunately, we have too many large corporations who oppress the majority of American people from seeking financial freedom. But fortunately, we also have these large corporations where we can, through the capital market, invest a tiny amount of money periodically to reach a level where money can work for us by producing passive income. So that we will never need to work with our labor anymore, we will discuss more on this topic in chapters 7, 8, and 9.

As you can see, these two solutions are interconnected with each other. One, we need to adjust our inner world first to be able to save enough money, which becomes capital. Hence, we will have more capital to participate in this system to help us gain real freedom- financial freedom. In other words, consumerism and materialism would take away our ability to benefit from the bright side of this rigged system.

Chapter 4
Financial Freedom

America is among the richest nations the world has ever seen. As far as its citizens are concerned, that wealth does not reach its citizens. American citizens are anything but richer compared to others on the global forum.

Essentially, Americans are no happier today than the generation in the 1950s. At the time, the income bracket and wealth were remarkably lower despite adjustment after inflation and median level.

Interestingly, a Gallup poll comprising 150,000 individuals from 140 countries discovered that forty-five Americans felt worried. While the global average was thirty-nine percent, Americans stood at an alarming forty-five percent.

If that was not all, the same Americans also felt stress excessively, standing at fifty-five percent. The remainder of the world was markedly lower, standing at thirty-five percent.

The difference here is that previously, we could make big purchases from our wealth. Purchasing bigger and better stuff became easier. However, we have relinquished control of our money over time.

The medium family income in 1955 was $29,000, whereas it was $62,000 in 2019. Our wealth has brought us to live a lifestyle hardly conceivable by the 1950s population, even for a median family. Furthermore, the median home grew when

we factor in the 1950s and 2018 numbers. Today, an average American home is larger and has more bathrooms than tenants.
Our LED televisions are sharp, our cars are more fuel-efficient and tech-savvy, and the internet has made nearly everything accessible.

Yet something is amiss here. Americans are still no better than they were in the 1950s.

Americans, for the most part, must taste financial freedom to enter the ranks of other nations. Presently, they are involved in a tiresome rat race that leaves them stressed out, pressurized and exhausted.

"The highest form of wealth is the ability to wake up every morning and say, "I can do whatever I want today." (Morgan Housel)

This is the central idea of my chapter, which sounds simple, yet requires careful short-term and long-term financial planning to get there.

Living in a capitalistic society, we may think at one point of living a financially-free life. When I say financially free, it means living with a mindset that no longer requires thinking about money every living hour of the day.

In this setup, money is no longer a part of the equation. You have enough of it to focus on other things. After all, life has bigger goals, which could be personal and professional ones. We are so bound by financial constraints to pay heed to other things.

Being financially free should be a top goal for most Americans stuck in the rat race. However, financially free and financial security are two different things.
One should not be confused with the other.

Financial security can vary for people depending on their age, phase of life, lifestyle, liabilities, and above all, goals and dreams. The recent pandemic affected people's financial security, who had to break the bank or use other forms of funds when the going became tough. The pandemic changed all that as our ability to manage, save and spend money underwent a marked change. Financial security did not assist as much as financial freedom would in pandemic-prone times. So, financial security means having money to cover the base expenses to support your lifestyle. It implies that your head is above the water, but you are still vulnerable.

In the section below, I will explore financial freedom and financial security and narrate instances separating the two:

Financial Security vs. Financial Freedom

Being financially free and financially secure are two different things. We will examine both individually.

Financial Security

People often think that being a multi-millionaire or a millionaire promises financial security. This is a misconception and further from the truth. Instances of athletes, entrepreneurs, and movie stars have made it abundantly clear that making a fortune is one thing and losing it all is another. Financial security is not everlasting. It can come crashing down quite quickly as well.

Financial security does not imply owning a mansion, a private jet, a Ferrari, or having paid off the entire mortgage on that summer house by the lake.

Financial security means you are in control of the money and have less to worry about the bill payment and covering some emergencies. Research shows financial security is understood as having the ability to live a modest lifestyle and comfortably postretirement. And more to the point, the financial requirements vary for either lifestyle and come at different costs.

Financial security means covering your base expenses, financial emergencies, and income adequate to map out future goals. Regardless of age and income bracket, financially secure individuals can support a certain living standard presently and in the future. Money is not necessarily a cause of undue stress in this case. However, financial security is vulnerable to market forces. External elements like the interest rates, economy, and government benefits may play a role in your financial security.

The phrase financial security may mean different things to different people. The four forms of financial security are listed below:
- Being debt-free
- Being in control of the money

- Prepared for emergencies
- Raising financial security

And still, it is vastly different from the financial freedom we will examine below.

Example Of Financial Security: I Cleared My Student Loans in Under Three Years

Jake Sexton was a marketing and communications specialist based in Indianapolis. He was drowning under twenty-eight thousand dollars of student loans. One day he finally decided to clear his outstanding debt and live a debt-free life moving forward. Jake paid off this debt in under three years while working a job that paid thirty thousand dollars per annum. He made it a routine to allocate half of the take-home income for his debt.

But the three years he was paying off loans, his friends would be out and about socializing and stuff, much to his envy. However, he had to bite the bullet to live a debt-free life. His life was greatly limited during the time he was paying off loans.

Moving forward, Jake and his wife have an emergency fund for unexpected situations and other economic challenges they will eventually face in due time. They also contribute to the retirement accounts with a ten percent amount every month.

The financial freedom they have as a married couple is greatly liberating. They do not fixate on money as much. For instance, if the dog becomes sick, they can visit a vet and have their pet treated quickly without worrying about the vet bills. Also, vacations are easy to plan and enjoy compared to before.

It felt extremely liberating when the day arrived; he had only one outstanding payment to make, clearing his student loans.

For Jake and his wife, money is no longer a priority. They have mapped out other goals they hope to pursue without thinking twice about the money.

Example Of Financial Security: I Cleared Debt Before Tying the Knot

Christina Markus was a public relations executive in her mid-30s. She was based in Maui, Hawaii, a popular tourist destination. Previously, she lived in San Diego, California, and relocated to the Hawaiian city in her mid-20s. She was under massive debt then, thanks to humongous college loans, overspending on vacations, and sharing accommodation space with her pals.

Making a move to Maui was the best decision of her life. Despite the higher cost of living in Maui, she discovered that the lifestyle is more affordable than in San Diego. Pricey dinners, nightly cocktails, and weekend getaways to Las Vegas and Palm Springs became a thing of the past. Her free time was more diverted to hiking, spending time with friends, and beaching. Without the higher cost, she enjoyed the same emotional satisfaction. In this way, she could enjoy life much more at a remarkably lesser cost.

I focused on the monthly minimums on my debt, and in a few years, I had cleared the debt on the car. My initial plan was to own a car. However, I was soon engaged to someone better than me in finances. My fiancée was very smart with his money management and never owed debt in his life. It was embarrassing that she was the one bringing debt to the marriage, which was a hefty sum of thirty thousand dollars. This strengthened her resolve to pay off her debts before the big day arrived. So, she had a time frame of two years to clear this debt.

I set up automatic transfers for loan payments from my account. During grocery runs, I only did the essential shopping. Times were tight, but she eventually paid off the debt a few months before the wedding. Thus, she tied the knot guilt-free.

The initial aim was to clear the debt. However, the whole experience taught her to be smart with the money moving forward. Her spending habits changed from that point. They have recently begun planning a New Zealand trip with a budget in place.

Financial Freedom

Financial freedom implies living life on your terms. The famed Roman philosopher Cicero has stated this precisely:

What then is freedom? The power to live as one wishes.

Again, this can mean different things to different people. Financial freedom depends on your innermost desires, be it early retirement, affording lavish travels, luxury purchases, or the capacity to leave a job without a worry in the world.

So, we must understand that financial security is achieved before financial freedom is attained. You cannot have one without the other.

People have an inherent desire to be wealthier, ultimately becoming happier. We must understand that happiness is a complex subject and may mean different things to different people. Though pigeonhole this happiness into a universal truth— a common denominator that unites us all.

Happiness is when people can control their lives. Happiness derives when we dictate the direction our life can take. The ability to do anything you want and whenever you want is the highest level of happiness. Furthermore, the leeway to do something for as long as one wants is also the highest form of happiness and priceless at the same time.

Example Of Financial Freedom: Henry Blake Quits his Job

This one individual named Henry Blake was working in midtown Manhattan at twenty thousand dollars per annum. It was minimum wage, to say the least. However, Henry lived a bare minimum life. He never dined out nor hailed a cab. In doing so, he brought his cost of living to a thousand dollars a month while earning eighteen hundred dollars a month. The difference of eight hundred dollars went into his saving. He kept saving for over two years until he had twelve thousand dollars in his savings account.

At the time, he was only twenty-two years old.

Reaching his desired benchmark, he quit his day job in Manhattan and became a full-time musician. He had realized that scoring a few gigs every month was more than enough to pay for his finances. He was free when he resigned from his placement and never retook a job placement.

When he narrated the story to his friend, his friend asked about the time he sold off his company for a higher ask. Henry just shrugged and said that was more money in the bank. That was the long and short of it. It did not make a marked difference in his life. The difference was when he quit his job and became a full-time musician.

Example of Financial Freedom: Learning The Value Of Investments

Gordon Brown was a test engineer in his mid-30s based in Michigan.

He and his wife had long decided to retire early and enjoy the finer things in life. After all, many people can earn and spend much of their waking hours working for someone else. It seems counterproductive and takes a vast chunk of their life, leaving little for themselves.

Thus, the plan was to accumulate investments over ten years and enjoy life. This was a ten-year plan. During a conversation about moving, they decided to recheck their financial status to take stock of the situation. If their incomes were good enough, they could defer it to a mortgage and make a move later.

To their surprise, they discovered that the investments are nearly seven hundred thousand dollars in stock, cash, and mutual funds. They crunched the number further and were surprised that the investment and retirement funds would still compound and hit their targeted number in due time if they pulled out right now. The nest egg would be a generous sum of just over one million, helping them take early retirement.

Simply put, the money they had invested was on a path of perpetual growth, irrespective of whether they were still investing or pulling out from it.

This brought forth a powerful sense of relief and surprise. They no longer had to be a part of the system to get out of it since they had made smart decisions prior, which led them here.

Resultantly, they felt good about themselves and their work thus far, boosting their confidence for the future, too.

Example of Financial Freedom: Life in a New Country Across the Ocean

In another life, Alex was a career-oriented man who was employed at a law firm and drew a six-figure salary. Taking early retirement, he relocated to Portugal with his wife at forty-one. They moved in 2011 after he had taken a vacation in the European country and found solace here.

Alex had moved here four years earlier while his wife moved to Portugal later. She was working as a nurse back in the U.S. Now they had officially retired.

When they hung their boots, their portfolio had highyielding stocks and funds, amounting to nearly one hundred and thirty thousand dollars each year. This covered their cost of living in the nation's capital, Washington DC.

Since they both loved Portugal, they decided to rent their apartment and move to Lisbon. This greatly cut their expenditures. More so, the amount from the rent was also reinvested into dividend-paying investment schemes, resulting in a compounded passive income stream.

It has been six years since they moved there, and life has become so much better now. Yet, they do not plan on relocating again because life is all set here. Listed below are expenditures they incur every month and the reason that makes life in Portugal so worth living.

Amazingly, the living expenses are remarkably low than in America. As is the case, Portugal is considered a low-cost country in the western bloc. Their expenses have declined by almost fifty percent now. They bought an apartment in Portugal that cost around €500,000 in 2015. It has an area of thirteen hundred square feet. This apartment has no mortgage at all.

So here is a breakdown of their expenses:

- Housing (property tax, insurance, and maintenance) $430
- Water and electricity: $175
- Phone and internet: $80
- Health Insurance (for the entire family) $258
- Groceries: $407
- Household essentials: $250
- Public transportation (gas, car, insurance, public transport): $250
- Dining out (ten to twelve meals per month): $600 This amounts to a total of $2450

Based in Lisbon, Portugal's capital, now it has changed its view of life and priorities. The two have also streamlined their worldly possessions after moving here. The focus is largely on how they spend the remainder of their days. For Alex, nature provides him with the inner satisfaction he had in mind. Taking strolls along the seashore at Guincho Beach is something he adores, while a hiking trip through the eucalyptus forests in the Colares and Sintra hills is always something to look forward to. Alex loves taking time out for his family. Occasional trips to Europe and sightseeing are their most valuable asset.

In conclusion, Alex has remained busy saving and investing his money, which helps him generate a decent cash flow. This allows him to have some financial freedom and control over his time. He is living in his favorite, idyllic spot where he can spend his retirement in full swing and the financial freedom he has attained by establishing a system that works for him.

Example of Financial Freedom: John D. Rockefeller

He was an American magnate and arguably the richest individual in the history of America. Rockefeller, during his meetings, would be silent. When one asked about the reason for his silence, he recited a poem: A wise old owl lived in an oak,

The more he saw, the less he spoke, the less he spoke, the more he heard. Why aren't we all like that wise old bird? Why aren't we all like that wise old bird?

Having secured financial freedom, Rockefeller was left with a wide array of thoughts that had less to do with his finances and money at the bank. His job was not to drill wells, load the trains or move the barrels. He made good decisions. It was not what he did with his bare hands or words. His most important was his mind and what went in his head. It was where he spent the bulk of his time. As a result, he would spend most of his hours and energy looking at the bigger picture. While things may seem different to others, he was constantly working in his mind. He had reached financial freedom where the money worked for him, leaving him to his devices.

This level of financial freedom was new to America and unique. In his day and age, most jobs required hands for completion. In 1870, forty-six percent and thirty-five jobs were in agriculture and manufacturing. Few professions solely relied on the mind of a person.

Benefits of Financial Freedom

When we attain financial freedom, the benefits are enjoyable on several levels. Some of the benefits are tangible, whereas the others are intangible yet equally important:

Beyond Daily Pressures

The psychological pressures of student loans and sky-high credit card debt can tax the human mind. It takes time, effort, and exhaustive stress later to clear it all away. Debt controls people and their actions and thoughts. It hampers their thoughts on other things they can do and enjoy.

Once we become debt-free and meet the required goals, crippling anxiety is replaced by peace, joy, and higher goals. You are now free to try new things in life and enjoy the experiences that matter most.

When you achieve financial freedom, you become enlightened and grow further.

Higher Fulfillment

With money in the bank, you have the leeway to take further risks that others cannot. With financial freedom, you are relaxed about meeting miscellaneous financial obligations. Since the money is already there, you are free to do other stuff and pursue things that demand your attention. In the back of your mind, you fully know that you can also deal with the consequences.

That is one of the perks of financial freedom.

Financial freedom means one can make bolder and more courageous decisions. You can pivot your lifestyle in healthier and more productive directions. You can quit that dreaded job, hectic working hours, or toxic work culture with financial freedom. Feats of this nature are possible only with cash cushions.

More Risks

The world is your oyster once you have gained financial freedom. It is like the floodgates of opportunities have opened to you right off the bat.

Some decide to relocate to a different country or part of the country. Others decide to live the rest of their days in the countryside. When one is not tied to a day job or a location, there are plenty of adventures and risks at your disposal.

When you know you are no longer to your next pay cheque, the fun truly begins.

How Much Money Ensures Financial Freedom?

This is the good part. There is no fixed amount that a person should reach to gain financial freedom. The right amount depends on the individual and their lifestyle aspirations.

As a rule of thumb, the money required to attain financial freedom is based on your annual expenses and income. Applying the 'multiply-by-25 rule' is a viable guide to saving for retirement. The same rule is also applicable to financial freedom as well.

The formula is mentioned below:

Financial freedom (quantity) = expected annual income x 25

So, for instance, a person needs fifty thousand dollars to live the desired lifestyle. Using the formula, the net amount for financial freedom would be $1.25 million (twenty-five multiplied by fifty-thousand dollars).

Aside from regular salary savings, the money can be increased further by compound interest, 401(k) employer matches, investments, and other passive income sources.

Should you pay off your mortgage first? We've discussed the purpose of saving money, which is to buy you freedom and control over your life and time. However, should you pay off your mortgage and other large debts first? Let's say you have $300000 on your bank account and a mortgage with a balance of $250k at the same bank. One day when you walk into the bank and ask a banker or financial advisor to give you this advice:" should I take that $300k to pay off my mortgage or do something with the money." I guarantee you that any bank personnel will tell you this:" well, over time stock market, for example, S&P 500, can provide you an average 9% return per year. In contrast, the mortgage is around 4%, so no brainer that you should meet our financial advisor and invest the money while keeping your mortgage." This is the way how banks can make money from you.

On the one hand, they can charge you about 3% overall fees on your investment portfolio. On the other hand, you will continue to pay interest on your mortgage. If you use the money to pay off the mortgage, the bank will lose money on both ends. Even though their advice is not wrong financially, the bank or anyone usually puts their interest before yours.

In my case, I paid off my mortgage. Remember, the equation of financial freedom is passive income - monthly expenses. At least 50% of Americans' expense is various loan payments: mortgage, car loan, student loans, and credit card debts. If you can apply your savings to pay off these debts, you would need much less passive income to reach financial freedom. The bankers and financial advisors give you their financial advice based on pure financial consideration. But very often, being financially free and happy is psychological consideration. Even though overtime S&P 500 provides an average of 9% return, this is before fees. Even if you invest in low-cost ETFs, you must consider the market downturn. There will guarantee to be a period of market downturn and crash. When your portfolio is down 1530%, your loan and mortgage payment will remain the same. In this case, you will very likely feel very stressed. If your wealth has significantly dropped while your fixed expense remains the same, you wouldn't feel good. All the stress, anxiety, and sense of uncertainty will lower the quality of your life. Remember, life is so short. It consists of every minute and second. When you invest a vast amount of your money while still paying a monthly payment, when markets drop significantly, you suffer double stress.

This is the main psychological reason I choose to pay off my mortgage and all debts before I invest my money. This way, my monthly overhead is reduced by at least 50%. Whenever my investment portfolio is down a lot, I can always remind myself that I have already reached semi-financial freedom, have paid off my debts, and don't need to use the investment money for the long-term, so I am OK."

Being financially free doesn't mean it has to be 100%. The whole thing relies on the equation of passive income - expenses. The more cost you can cut, the closer you are to financial freedom. Let's say your overhead is $5000 per month, and your passive income is $3000 per month. In this case, even though you have not fully reached financial freedom, at least you have reached 60% financial freedom. That means you still have way more control over your time than most people. Though you still have to work to fill the gap, you can work fewer hours, find a job that doesn't pay well but is something you genuinely want to do, or have more power to say no to your employers. Reaching 50% of financial freedom is not bad. This gives you balance in life. You can work probably 20 hours a week, that at least gives you something to do. Those who can fully retire often find life boring and meaningless.

Therefore, you must always stick with your goal of reaching financial freedom. To do so, you need to play offense and defense. The defense part is simple: pay off your debts and reduce expenses.

Be that as it may, financial freedom may sound different to everyone. For some people, it may be a debt-free life with sufficient money in the bank to live comfortably. For others, financial freedom means caring for their children or loved ones without monetary constraints. Maybe it has enough money to retire early.

Regardless of your definition of financial freedom, its rewards outweigh the economic confines. The psychological payoff is equally valuable.

Thus, the freedom to select what you wish to do with your time is unlike any other. The pursuits could be a great many and of one's interest. The hours are chosen as per convenience.

Becoming financially free is the first day of the rest of your life. You are your own man, which means you set the terms and desires. The rest will fall into place by itself.

Chapter 5
Maslow's Hierarchy of Needs and Financial Freedom

Abraham Maslow was an American psychologist who presented a theory in his 1954 seminal book *Motivation and Personality*. Today, we know this model as Maslow's Hierarchy of Needs. The famed model has grown in popularity over the years and applied to several domains as well:

- Workplace application
- Financial application
- Personal application
- Collective application

The chapter will discuss the financial application of Maslow's Hierarchy of Needs and Financial Freedom in tow.

The theory professes to explain human motivation and ranks them in order of their priority. According to this model, some basic needs should be fulfilled before people can move on to more nuanced needs.

The famed model is usually known in the mainstream culture as a pyramid-shaped graph showcasing five levels of needs. We will discuss these models one by one below to demonstrate how they each represent a part of the lives we live every day:

- **Physiological needs:** These are lower-level needs and form a vast base of this pyramid. They may include food, water, clothing, rest, health, shelter, and reproduction. Maslow contends covering this level before moving to other levels above.

- **Safety needs:** These needs imply safety and security, which we need crucially. They include protection from violence, emotional stability, health security, well-being, and theft. The need will probably become important once we have acquired our physiological needs.

- **Love and belonging needs:** This need arises from the need to belong somewhere or be part of a group of people. This need will inevitably become necessary when the safety and physiological needs are fulfilled.

- **Esteem needs:** From this domain begins the higher order of needs, which are more ego-driven needs. The elements making this one involves self-respect and self-esteem. The former comes from a sense of being valuable, while the latter stems from confidence in abilities and accomplishments.

- **Self-actualization:** This is the highest stage that we must achieve. In this phase, we can move on to bigger and better life goals because the previous ones are now fulfilled. The individual can step on a path of real growth and achieve the ideal state in mind.

Growth Needs and Deficiency Needs

The American psychologist referred to self-actualization as a 'growth need,' which stands differently from all the other levels in the hierarchy. These lower level needs he calls 'deficiency needs' are different. Incidentally, if an individual fails to meet their deficiency needs, the results can be disastrous and harmful in some capacity. These may include loneliness, starvation, illness, and self-doubt when needs are unmet.

Interestingly, the self-actualization needs can make one happier than before and even empowered. However, they do not overtly cause any harm when they remain unfulfilled. Therefore, self-actualization is only prioritized when the foundational needs are fully met.

Roadmap to Financial Freedom and Maslow's Hierarchy of Needs Model

We have five levels of financial needs in terms of the model presented by the American psychologist Maslow:

1. **Cash flow and basic needs:** This covers the daily, housing, and food-related expenses. And more importantly, physiological needs are also covered in financial terms.
2. **Financial safety:** This may include emergency and insurance funds in order to deal with unforeseen events and other significant expenditures. This is more of a financial cushion that should cover a person for a few months when some major issue happens—it could be a car crash, health-related issue, or an impending recession.

3. **Accumulating wealth:** This area includes clearing debts, growing investments, and saving for retirement. The level majorly focuses on increasing the assets for long-lasting success.
4. **Financial freedom:** This is an important area and spells fiscal freedom for the individual. The self-esteem needs are also fulfilled by now, and one feels accomplished in this phase.
5. **Legacy:** Although this is subjective, ordinarily involving tax planning, real estate planning, and business succession planning come into this domain, completing the pyramid.

This is the roadmap for achieving long-term financial health and the goals of your choice. In the sections below, we will examine how some of the biggest names in the culture have achieved financial freedom and put their valuable time into valuable pursuits that shaped our way of life and thinking, for that matter.

Surpassing the Rat Race

The following are some markers of succumbing to the rat race and living in a consumer-oriented society for the most part. We must see the signs and break the shackles to reach self-actualization. Some of the areas holding you back in this regard might be the following:

- **Paycheck-to-paycheck Lifestyle:** Forcing yourself to live from one paycheck only to wait for the next paycheck means you will be caught in an unending cycle of clearing the outstanding payments in the form of credit card payments, utility bills, and other stuff.

Growing your investments and savings will strengthen your financial footing and eventually leave out this endless and torturous cycle. So, even if payments are delayed for some reason, then you have no worries regardless. You are still in your comfort zone. Therefore, breaking free of the paycheck-to-paycheck lifestyle is the first step in the right direction, offering stability like never before.

- **No Emergency Funds/Savings:** Our society has normalized saving absolutely nothing for a rainy day. This could mean that people are one paycheck away from filing for bankruptcy or something of the sort. Unfortunately, this happens more often than one thinks.

   Credit cards and lines of credit are not never-ending cash sources. They come with a timeline and certainly can be revoked at the next possible moment. Therefore, making them a lifeline is counterproductive, let alone accomplishing financial freedom.

- **Spending More than Earning:** If you habitually spend more than your earnings, then sooner than later, you will be in hot waters. People may often avoid this by adding debts to car loans, mortgages, or lines of credit. Unfortunately, this will simply solve an issue that you could have avoided in the first place. As a matter of fact, some lifestyle changes are in order before you step on the road to self-actualization. You have to make some changes in your budget so that you will spend less than you make. Otherwise, you are only delaying the inevitable. In order to work out the spending each month, take a pencil and paper and work out the details of the incoming cash flow and outgoing funds.

There are many more financial mistakes that you are committing (among these few) that are restraining you from reaching a future promising financial freedom.

Reflections on Self-Actualization

We spend a long life and do tons of stuff. However, we need to examine life from time to time. An unexamined life is not worth living either. Some people open their eyes and enter the rat race without rhyme or reason. The urge to succeed in life takes a life of its own and thus begins a lifelong race, sort of a trap, as life ebbs away in this self-imprisonment.

But then others value family above all, while a child may like ice cream flavor from some brand as the highest pursuit of life. An older woman may declare her legacy as the most important thing for her and her offspring. Be that as it may, people value things that make them happy, which means whatever makes them happy enough is valuable to them.

Some people may believe the present should make them happy without sacrificing tomorrow. This brings me to a timeless question, which remains universally disagreed upon all this time.

Can money buy happiness and the highest form of happiness?

Psychologists Angus Deaton and Daniel Kahneman have declared that money may buy happiness until we have reached the seventy-thousand-dollar benchmark. They opine that surpassing that amount of money has no actual impact. The dollar amount is arguable, but I suppose one can agree that we are happy when the essentials of life are fulfilled. The elements of cold, hunger, food, shelter, and security may give us sleepless nights. The absence of any of them can trouble our minds. We continue to foster an ecosystem where we have all of this and provide it to our family.

But life has so much more to offer than this. We are sidelining the aspects that matter most and should matter as well. Benjamin Franklin famously stated: Health is wealth.

Maybe irony died a hundred times here since Benjamin Franklin has his face imprinted on the American currency. But he had a point all this time. When we have to pursue greater goals in life and live higher aims, we certainly need to look past the greenback boogie.

And when we have achieved that, it is time to look at higher aims in life.

When freed from the rat race, we can focus on the things that matter most. For some people, financial freedom may begin on the eve of dawn. Their alarm clock goes off, and they wake up giddy for the day ahead. And in doing so, they rise and grind. As they put their feet on the ground, they know their day ahead is full of fresh possibilities and new openings.

A challenge of this sort is backed by immense passion. For instance, a person may find their battle an uphill one, yet they could be brimming with excitement and thrill. Their engagement makes them feel more energized and fulfilled from the inside. As a result, they experience a feeling unlike ever before. Sure, a healthy living, family life, and career running tandem still leave much to be desired.

For instance, the owner of a major bank has shareholders and a board of directors running the day-to-day operations of his company that he has set up after years of work. However, after setting up people in his place and running an entity that works without his involvement, he can now focus on self-improvement and self-actualization like never before. However, when the bank owner embarks on this journey, he has a new realization—he is merely scratching the surface here. The journey is long yet exciting and equally rewarding. So, I have something to say here.

There have been many individuals who have acquired the self-actualization stage. History is laden with figures that have soared above the confines of finances and implemented ideas/systems that they loved and wished to bring about a change on a micro/macro scale. And the change brought only goes to show the potential of self-actualization.

I believe there is more to Maslow's model than meets the eye:

- The Theory of Human Motivation thinks that people at the top are fulfilled, which I find paradoxical. When we reach self-actualization, we acquire more skills and realize that our ceiling has only become higher. So, that means we are far away from self-actualization than before. Reaching that previous benchmark was just the perceived notion of self-actualization. But not the actual self-actualization itself. So, the better we get over time, the better potential we must up the ante and push the envelope en route to self-actualization.

- Secondly, how is happiness guaranteed if there is a top and people are up there? The top of the pyramid is the basis for another long journey ahead. Those who have reached the pyramid's peak find more challenges ahead and maybe another pyramid awaiting them.

So, I would humbly wager that Maslow's Hierarchy of Needs should rarely be viewed as a one-size-fits-all solution when you have reached the self-actualization phase. Challenges have merely started when you reach that front. It is similar to an ascending staircase that may lead to a descending staircase and later ascend, consisting of both peaks and valleys.

Since the earth's creation, there have been an enormous number of organisms and lives; many of them have been extinct for billions of years. Even today, scientists estimate there are 8.7 million kinds of species. But only humans have the giant brain and the highest level of intelligence. So, we should wisely use money; that means not wasting too much money on pursuing animalistic items, such as materials, but living a more intellectual life. This universe and world are wonderful. We should do our best to achieve financial freedom by spending less money on obsessive material needs, so we can have more time to explore and experience this world since our time on this planet is short. Just in the human body, there are 100 trillion cells that make up our body; inside each cell, millions of objects work every second to make your existence possible. There are at least 100 billion stars in our galaxy and at least 100 billion galaxies in our observable universe. And how many universes are out there? We do not know. Only humans can use our brain and intellect to perceive and understand this magical and incredible universe. So why should we let ourselves become the slaves of money and keep hovering at the very bottom of human needs and pursuit? Instead, we should save money and reach financial freedom, though it doesn't have to be 100% financially free. The more financial freedom we get, the more time we can spend pursuing self-actualization or development.

    Let's look at this from another angle. We all live for two things: body and mind/soul. When we need essential foods, shelter, and other fundamental materials, we are dealing with our body/physiological needs. Nowadays, at least in America, most people already have an abundance of food, materials, and bigger shelters. But an existing survey has found that between 30%-90% of American adults experience boredom at some point in their daily lives. Another research reveals that the average adult experience 131 days of boredom a year. When our stomach is empty, we feel hungry, so we need to eat food. When our mind is empty, we thus think bored; we need to feed our minds with "foods" as well. So, the best food for the reason is intellectual curiosity, in other words, books, all kinds of books, traditional books, audiobooks, e-books, and YouTube educational channels. Intellectual curiosity is the best tool to fight against boredom. Let books be your best food to feed your mind's hunger. It is so easy to fill our stomachs today, but not always easy to fill our minds. That is why there are all kinds of psychological problems people are facing. Too many foods and materials make you unhealthy physiologically. Too little intellectual curiosity and books can make you harmful psychologically.

Reading books is an intimate process because you spend time alone with the innermost thoughts and feelings to perceive your mind and existence. According to Rene Descartes's most famous quote, I think I am. Reading books helps you to discover the world and people without leaving the house, not even leaving your chair. In conclusion, living for your body is a low-end of life pursuit. Living for your mind is more equivalent to realizing self-actualization and self-development. We, humans, are the only species on this planet that can use written language to write down our thoughts and ideas. So, we are the only beings who can chase a higher end of lifestyle. Saving more and reaching financial freedom is the prerequisite of living a higher-end, more valuable lifestyle.

Below are some individuals who reached financial freedom and then moved on to different challenges of their day and age. Interestingly, we can see their challenges continued erstwhile:

Voltaire and Financial Freedom

In his youthful days, Voltaire realized that he had to live a financially free life in order to achieve his aims and speak the truth. The thought of making a living was something counterproductive to his monumental ideals. Therefore, he set to work and befriended several people from the financial world. His new pals taught him investments in currencies and commodities and the art of managing money.

Soon enough, Voltaire had a circle of wealthy bankers, Paris brothers, and other professionals who gave valuable pearls of wisdom, making him a millionaire when he reached forty. He essentially owned 'a bank on the seas,' involved in trading and lending, supporting international trade.

Voltaire had funds invested in many parts of the world (we call them countries today), which helped him earn dividends, profits, and interest year-round. This system he had created to support himself for the rest of his day.

The system was well in place for him to live comfortably and escape when the times became hostile to him due to his social and political ideas. Moreover, in doing so, he also prevented himself from depending on a single economy. And in doing so, it also stirred a massive scandal since Voltaire was loyal to his kingship first and foremost.

This made Voltaire invest most of his focus as being one of the most influential French writers, making a name for himself due to his writings. Given most of his works are still unread, he stood as a shining figure against cruelty, bigotry, and tyranny. His satire and wit led to a change in Europe unlike any other.

Voltaire and Passive Income

When Voltaire was in his mid-50s, the secretary estimated that the famed author was earning a whopping sum of eight thousand francs annually, which equals six hundred thousand dollars in present money when adjusted for inflation. Aside from this, he earned an additional forty-five thousand francs annually from several passive investments globally. This translates to around three hundred and forty thousand dollars in present-day money.

And in net earnings, he made nearly a hundred dollars back in the day, thanks to his business acumen and financial literacy. This allowed him to live a comfortable life and pursue the higher aims in life, which were meaningful to him.

The passive earnings would arrive in his pockets while he criticized the French judicial system and opined on ideas about how the society should work and govern itself. He lived a comfortable life overall and died in peace as well. With his lifestyle and finances taken care of, he moved on to bigger and better things.

His contemporary, Mozart, was not so much lucky. The famed musician spent a vast chunk of his life in debt repayments and suing by friends for his outstanding debts.

Montesquieu and Financial Freedom

Montesquieu was born as Charles-Louis de Secondat. He belonged to a wealthy family, which helped him educate himself in one of the prestigious places in the country. His father, Jacques de Secondat, was a member of an old, modestly wealthy military family that had been knighted in the 16th century for services to the crown. At the same time, his mother, Marie-Francoise de Pesnel, was a devout lady of partial English descent. She brought her husband a substantial increase in wealth through La Brède's valuable wine-producing property. In 1715, he wed a wealthy Protestant woman named Jeanne de Lartigue. She brought him a good dowry of 100,000 Livres and gave him three children: two girls and a son named Jean-Baptiste. After his uncle Jean-Baptiste, Baron de Montesquieu, passed away in 1716, he bequeathed his possessions to his nephew. This included the barony of
Montesquieu, near Agen, as well as the role of deputy president in the Parlement of Bordeaux. His position carried a certain amount of prestige. It was not a sinecure, but it did come with a stipend. Other than that, he was renowned in the social circles of France. At 27, Montesquieu reached a point when he was socially and financially stable. He settled down to carry out his

judicial function (to this end, he engaged in the minute study of Roman law), administer his property, and advance his knowledge of the sciences, particularly geology, biology, and physics, which he studied in the newly formed Academy of Bordeaux. He did all these things simultaneously.

Interestingly, he lived in a period of significant change, and later, when he rose to fame in his local circles, his family wealth continued to support him through the rest of his years. Money was the last thing on his mind since he openly spoke and wrote on the social and political issues of the day to pursue the higher level of intellectual need- self-actualization. With high aims in mind, he worked on the broad ideals he believed in and propagated them.

The Spirit of Law is one of his most famous books. The idea of this great book has impacted western civilization till today. Though Montesquieu was born with and inherited great wealth, he has never used his great wealth to chase material wants and simple goals. Instead, his financial freedom and wealth allowed him to pursue the higher end of Maslow's hierarchy- self-actualization in the form of intellectual pursuit.

Einstein and His Intellectual Pursuit

It has been a hundred years since Albert Einstein first published the famed theory of general relativity. The theory essentially changed the way we see the universe today. And interestingly, our everyday life screams general relativity due to our massive reliance on these tech devices.

Nothing gave Einstein more empowerment and a sense of fulfillment than following his intellectual pursuits as a scientist. He worked for the betterment of humanity, thought of nations as one, and propagated his ideas to others around him.

Soon enough, after he published the theory of special relativity in 1905, he was still unsatisfied because he realized that it only applied to constant speed. However, there is merely any constant speed in our universe, especially gravity. Since he attempted to incorporate gravity into a general theory, he needed to develop a new approach. "I was sitting in a chair in the patent office at Bern when suddenly a thought occurred to me," he recalled. "If a person falls freely, he will not feel his weight." Once this realization came into his mind, he was shocked, which led him to hard work for the next eight years to develop and generalize his special theory of relativity into a theory of gravity. According to him, gravity is not a force that pulls objects together but rather a geometric property of curved space-time. As Einstein proudly summed up, it was his life's happiest thought.

As you can see, this is a great story that shows how a great human being can use a pure thought experiment to discover the secrets of the universe. In other words, it demonstrates that we humans possess the most wonderous equipment, our brain, that allows us to perceive and experience the wonder of the universe. The capability and feeling of pure thought experiments help us reach the highest level of internal happiness and satisfaction.

Maslow has provided a timeless model for achieving the highest form of human existence. While working through our lower-order needs, we can eventually reach the self-actualization phase, where we can pursue interests that we hold dear and add value to our life. It is all a matter of thinking differently. For instance, I will give an instance below:

The consumer mindset would think that money is spent in just one way. When we purchase products, materials, or services in exchange for money, ordinarily, we believe that is when we spend money. However, I see things slightly differently here. When we invest money or save it somewhere for later usage, we still spend money one way or the other. In this case, we are spending money to buy something bigger—self-esteem or maybe head towards self-actualization.

Without conscious investment in financial freedom, we will be stuck in the lower quadrants of Maslow's Hierarchy of Needs model. Likely, we may not surpass the third level of the pyramid herein.

Therefore, the model is a step in the right direction as far as financial freedom and self-actualization are concerned.

Chapter 6
The Simpler The Better Lifestyle

Our lives should revolve around one maxim that should have an overarching effect.

'Keep it simple, stupid.'

Though simple, the one line says so much about life itself. We need to keep things simple because simple is good. Simple works!

Be it products, processes, or explanations, people will always prefer the simplest things out there because it works for them as it works for others.

In hindsight, the catchphrase 'keep it simple, stupid' applies to so much more.

Kelly Johnson was allegedly the first individual, a lead engineer at Lockheed Skunk Works, who first came up with this catchphrase.

He told his design engineers at the company that whatever they implemented should be simple enough for an average man in the field to repair with simple tools and mechanic training. Lockheed was front and center in the war theatre then, which meant if the products were not simple enough, they would soon be unfavorable for combat conditions, rendering the company entirely worthless.

Today, the famed KISS principle is widely applied almost everywhere, finding its use beyond the engineering domain. We see it in management, design areas, software engineering, trainers and educators, and workplace domains just the same.

So, simplicity is king.

Interestingly, Steve Jobs pioneered simplistic design. For him, simplicity was everything. His focus over the years (be it iPod, Macintosh, or iPhones) was promising simplicity in everything the company offered, elevating simplicity to an art form. According to him, it was hard work to make something challenging and yet come up with elegant solutions. Thus, simplicity was the ultimate sophistication, all things considered.

However, Steve Jobs from the tech world is not the only high-profile individual who believes in simplicity at the core. We now turn to the financial world.

Warren Buffet, a legendary investor, opines investment is a simple game, which financial advisors have truly oversold people as the stuff of nightmares and cosmic dangers.

Warren Buffet has seen wars, economic depressions, and political scandals, among so much more. Yet, his strategy from day one has remained the same since the day he started. He had bought high-quality companies when they were at their lowest point, buying them out for dirt-cheap prices. The key is to avoid them when they are at a high in the market.

Since the dawn of time, Buffet has invested with this principle in mind. For him, a share is a portion of the business instead of a gambling chip at a casino. He analyzes the company and sees how much the firm is worth before investing. The rest of the market is immaterial to him as he works in his old-school fashion.

The strategy is simple as it gets—the aim is to buy businesses rather than stocks. Warren does not predict the future or outfox the competition here. Investing in a sound business is the key here; that is all his strategy is.

It is so simple that Buffet believes that most investors can replicate and even children can do this while at school.

Therefore, at the heart of Buffet's strategy is old fashioned simplicity.

Simplicity should be adopted as a principle in life. The easier something is, the more likelihood is there for its adoption. We can use the KISS strategy in life and finances as well. After all, sometimes, the answers are the simplest.

Our life and finances are no different in this regard. We must keep it simple and avoid the entanglements herein.

Enter the Minimalist Lifestyle

The term minimalism applies to just about everything. This term as a concept directly challenges our consumer and capitalist society at hand. It helps establish mental clarity by steering clear from materialistic possessions. The minimalists like things simple and easy.
That is the long and short of it.

Minimalists prefer nature over everything, opting for human experiences rather than accumulating superficial items for self-indulgence. They will prefer traveling and visiting new spots to being tied to a desk job all day with back pain.

The core aim of the minimalists is that all the material possessions in our lives, thanks to capitalism, will never make us truly happy. When we do that, we move away from our primal instincts and things that truly make us happy.

The concept deeply applies to the American way of life— and for a good reason. We see people in Scandinavian countries and how much they value life. Their work-life balance is well controlled, helping them explore life and things that make them feel fulfilled.

On the other hand, we have the American lifestyle raging with discontent, stress, frustration, and piles of debt in tow. Americans fall into the rabbit hole of consumerism and begin to descend deeper and deeper. In their pursuit of happiness, they merely widen the hole of misery and discontent in their lives by adding debt to their name and compounding mental stress and physical exertion.

Thorstein Veblen, an economist, coined the term "conspicuous consumption" in 1899. This phrase referred to wealthy upper-class individuals obsessed with displaying their identity and social status by purchasing and possessing numerous luxury items, such as jewelry, watches, etc. At the time, only a few wealthy individuals could afford such conspicuous consumption. With the explosion of information technology, almost everyone now has a specific consumption capability, and this conspicuous consumption has intensified. The media relentlessly promote the notion that possessing and consuming more signifies a higher social status and a prosperous life. Flaunting your newly acquired items on social media to spur envy and admiration from your friends is a sign of success. However, this is an illusion you maintain for the benefit of others, not yourself. In exchange, you lose significant freedom. You may be extremely busy all day but feel empty and superficial. Therefore, living a simpler life can help you regain physical and mental freedom.

The good news is that a bulk of this mental and physical baggage can be brought down and eliminated. Commodity fetishism has plagued American society and stained its social fabric. So, if an average American can well understand that their life has more than material possessions, they can free themselves from the perils and horrors of commodity fetishism.

Karl Marx, the famed German philosopher, maintained that people see the product of labor as the relationship between things instead of social relationships with people. Therefore, people see the commodity in terms of the product, whereas the creation process remains obscure and beyond consideration.

An Analysis of Consumerist and Minimalist Lifestyles

The famed Chinese hermit Xu You once observed a mole sipping water from a pond. He then learned that when the mole is thirsty, it only drinks a bellyful, no more, no less, but precisely what it requires. The mole does not burden itself with excesses since doing so would impede its movement, unlike humans, who frequently consume far more than they need. We may not drink too much water, but we often overwhelm ourselves with material possessions, purchasing far more than we require to live and thrive. Consumerism has a cost since it demands resources to stay up with other consumers. As a result, many individuals are prepared to work themselves to the grave and acquire what we might call extensions of themselves or their egos. They tend to believe that since I have more, I am more. As a result, accumulating their stuff increases their feeling of self. Emperor Yao admired the reclusive Xu You so much that he was willing to hand over his throne to him. However, Xu You (who lived as a hermit and calm life by the river) declined, telling the emperor that he did not need all under heaven and said, "When the tailorbird makes her nest in the deep wood, she needs no more than one branch." The hermit who lives in poverty is given something that many others can only dream of command over the entire kingdom. But he preferred to live as a hermit in a remote location. The less you possess, the less you may lose, and the less you must worry about, giving you more freedom to live your life to the utmost. As a result, the simpler living principle is that less is more.

Essentially, the minimalist lifestyle is a retaliation to the massively popular consumerist society. As is the case, capitalism thrives on consumerism for its survival. So, we can say that capitalism will last as long as consumerism reigns supreme. Indeed! Capitalism is an economic system fueled by raging consumerism and, in some cases, extreme consumerism.

And yes, this is not some conspiracy theory or anticapitalistic rhetoric. This is a plain fact, and economists will unanimously agree with it. So, upon some analysis, you will reach these conclusions:

- Water is wet
- Gravity keeps us on the ground
- Capitalism needs consumerism to thrive (the more, the better)

So, there you have it. We live a consumer-driven life, thrown into a whirlwind with no end in sight. Is that the life you want? Think about this long and hard.

Interestingly, the minimalist lifestyle is nothing new. It is as old as the man himself. Religion, spirituality, and creatives from several fields—have all talked about the perils of materialism. From the days of yore, shamans, monks, priests, gurus, hermits, and artists of different degrees have mostly eschewed possessions.

Even religions have identified the distraction due to material wealth/possessions and its dangers. Jesus has famously said: The love of money is the root of all evil.

Another instance is the hippies who proposed counterculture. This happy-go-lucky gang of the 1960s had adopted a mantra *turn on, tune in, drop out*, which was a drug reference. But it also encouraged an alternate lifestyle that revolved around minimalism and self-awareness. Back then, the hipster generation had made a move to shy away from mainstream consumerism and switched to recycling, repurposing, and avoiding purchasing.

All these different voices through time stood against capitalism for a reason.

Under capitalism, we are liable to see a systematic disruption and change of our social fabric and environmental change. It has heralded a wave of counterintuitive change to our inner selves.

Minimalism can change the nature of production and have a good impact on the environment as well. But the effects are more than physical and environmental.

When we let go of capitalism and all the vices it does bring; we also feel incredibly free. The mental clutter and excursion due to capitalism and consumerism take the exit door itself, relieving a burden off the shoulders. Incidentally, holding onto things mentally and emotionally often weighs us down, which is a byproduct of this lifestyle.

So, if we can use the right tools and methods to focus our efforts on reducing the clutter in our lives within a short time frame, the results will become instantly clear, allowing you to have much more breathing space.

Minimalism involves removing the needless items from the equation and focusing on the good stuff that matters. The concept challenges consumerist culture, allowing people to transition on the right track by emphasizing experiences over material possessions.

Resultantly, minimalism as a lifestyle can help us reclaim our time and discover life's true meaning. It is time high time we pursue our passions and live every moment as the best we can. In doing so, we will undoubtedly reclaim the spiritual energy that the capitalist and consumerist society have robbed us.

Instances of Minimalist Lifestyle Adoption

- We have some real-life instances in this case as well. Take the case of Ryan Nicodemus and Joshua Fields, who cowrote the bestselling book titled *The Minimalism: A Meaning Life.* In their first book, they avidly talk about a time when they were young urban professionals based in Dayton, Ohio. The boys had a six-figure salary and lived a life that they wanted. From fancy cars, branded outfits, big houses, and plenty of fun stuff to keep them occupied—they had an empty feeling inside. Something was amiss here. All the money in the world and this glitzy lifestyle still were not enough for true happiness. They felt dissatisfied with life, and that sinking feeling was still mostly there. Working seventy to eighty hours weekly and riding a high wave of the consumerist society still failed to fill the void inside them. Rather, the void was getting wider and wider. They reflected on their lifestyle choices and decided to make some much-needed changes. As a result, they adopted minimalism in their lives and decided to see what was more important in life—the aim here was to focus on self-development and grow as a person.

- We take the instance of Morgan Housel, the renowned author of the book, *The Psychology of Money,* who has similar feelings on the matter. Acquiring an intern job placement at a major investment bank, he was pleasantly surprised by the employees' work ethic. Soon enough, he realized these bankers' whopping amount of money annually. They had long working hours, which were controlled heavily by their higher-ups. It was his first stint at the investment bank, and he was surprised to see the days of their lives people put in there. Heading home before midnight was deemed as a luxury for them, chances of which were far and few. A famous line at this office was: *If you do not arrive at work on Saturday, you might as well avoid coming on Sunday.* This job paid big bucks, and certainly as one got their money's worth here. But for what? The prime years of your life would certainly go down the drain when wealth was there to leave the bank for good. Our author, Morgan, seemed drained out from the demanding job and pandering to the bank's whims, resulting in his life's horrid experiences. The four-month internship was reduced to only one month, which

is why he now has a minimalist stance on life. He proposes saving money, living a frugal life, and keeping things simple.

- Leo Babauta, the creator of the website Zen Habit, is another excellent example. When he was 35, his life was in disarray. He was overweight, a smoker, and in significant debt. Finally, he was determined to simplify his life. By implementing nine rules for a clearer day, he could quit smoking, lose over 60 pounds, eliminate debt, become an entrepreneur, and raise six children within a few years. Time Magazine ranked its Zen Habit website among the top 50 websites of that year. Therefore, a simpler lifestyle facilitates financial freedom and improves health. Once you achieve financial freedom, you will have the time to pursue things that are more important to you.
- Steve Jobs once stated that he prefers a minimalistic approach to his personal and professional life. From 1998 to 2010, he wore only a black shirt and blue jeans in virtually all his photographs taken on different occasions. When he was in his thirties, the only items in his home were a portrait of Albert Einstein, a lamp, a chair, and a bed. Almost no furniture. Steve Jobs has adhered to this philosophy throughout his life: less is more. Yes, he had a great deal of money.

For years, Mark Zuckerberg has been another excellent example of living a simple life; he has worn only a gray shirt and blue jeans. People even wonder if he ever takes a shower. He said: "Based on psychological theory, he tries to avoid wasting time on unimportant activities." Choosing what to wear and what to eat every day, as well as other trivial matters, consumes a significant amount of energy and makes me feel as if I am not working toward meaningful pursuits and objectives. Connecting 1 billion individuals is essential to me." This is a beautiful example of adapting to a simpler lifestyle and not wasting time on superficial materialism to pursue what is important to you. This principle applies to life itself—Minimalism can liberate us from the shackles of capitalism. It can play a decisive role in changing our life on its head by offering and introducing new elements capitalism cannot promise.

Maybe the best answers in life are simple. And perhaps, just maybe, we have found our true calling in doing so.

A common Chinese proverb from Confucius declares *Wuyuzegang* (无欲则刚)—the translation goes like this: One can be strong if they do not have desires. This roughly means living a life with minimum desires. After all, we are victims of our desires and give in moments of weakness.

When we comprehensively adopt minimalism as a lifestyle, we will likely steer away from the capitalism trap.

Steering Clear of Material Possessions

This quote from Ryan Nicodemus and Joshua Fields seems appropriate here:

Minimalism is a tool that can assist you in finding freedom. Freedom from fear. Freedom from worry. Freedom from overwhelm. Freedom from guilt. Freedom from depression. Freedom from the trappings of the consumer culture we've built our lives around. Real freedom.

Interestingly, we should understand that one aspect of minimalism is cutting down possessions and material wealth. However, this principle is not central to it.

Be that as it may, the minimalist lifestyle is less concerned about how much we own and is geared more towards attitudes governing the following:

- Stuff we own
- Stuff we do not own
- Stuff we wish to own

Therefore, successful minimalism is not necessarily owning a select few items and being content with them.

There is a large force at play here that we need to understand.

The Minimalist Focus

When it comes to consumerism does a great job of focusing our attention, activities, and energies on materialism. The consumerist culture pushes us into buying more stuff and then more stuff. We are circling in a whirlpool of using, buying, and replacing stuff, and the cycle continues.

We often think that relationships, family, and people hold more value in life than material possession. But our behavior shows otherwise. Therefore, our stated philosophy is pretty way off the mark from the practical application:

Here are some instances:

- Notice the time we spend at work and put it in contrast to time spent with real people (friends, family, and others)
- After office hours, notice the time spent on handheld devices and electronic items instead of holding a conversation with people close to you
- Notice the time we spend on purchasing stuff we want
- Notice the amount of information you have on the latest gizmos on the market
- Do you set money aside for future purchases?
- Do you have stuff you purchased during impulsive buying that remains unused?

I do not aim to judge you or criticize you for these behaviors. We have all been guilty of this behavior at one point or the other. After all, are we not products of this society, and does not our culture revolve around material possessions? We are trapped in this cycle:

- Want it
- Research it
- Purchase it
- Use it
- Replace it

Consumerism is ingrained in us since we have opened our eyes to, lived, and breathed it.

The fault lies in the stated philosophy and our inconsistency in carrying it out. The things we do not have, we want them and work hard to get them. Once we have them, we will begin our romance with the next thing in the line-up. As consumers, we want stuff, and therein lies our primary focus.

The Aim of Minimalism

The larger aim is to align our focus with the stated philosophy. Minimalism shifts our focus from things to people. It allows us to look at health, art, activities, and our passion.

It shifts us from the consuming mindset to creating instead, allowing us to enjoy in the true sense of the word.

True minimalism does not simply involve stripping ourselves of our prized possessions. It also stresses the importance of refocusing the priorities, realizing our priorities, and avoidance of stuff that poses a significant distraction from the bigger picture that is more valuable.

Minimalism Back in Childhood

Now let us take a trip down memory lane and recall our childhood days. Most of our material possessions in the early twenties could easily fit into a rucksack or a suitcase. We did not own as much back then, and surprisingly, we did not need as much to live.

So, you can remember that we lived well back then.

Those were different times back then, and I am sure you will understand that life did not revolve around material possessions much.

And yes, our focus in life was different and largely uninvolved with material possessions.

Putting it Into Practice

From the days of yore comes Henry David Thoreau, an American naturalist. He showed the perfect instance to live a simple life and be happy while he was at it. His life was simple yet gave huge meaning to his well-being.

The author of the book *Walden and Civil Disobedience* is a highly recommended read by English professors in academic institutes.

Interestingly, Thoreau had a chance to analyze human psychology long before Maslow did. He emphasized in his book that we should live a humble and simple life, steering clear from addressing physiological needs. Once that has been accomplished, people can focus on self-development and take things from there.

Going through his philosophy, we can find inner peace, do some soul searching and reconsider our relationship with nature. He showed that humans fit well with animals, trees, and plants. His house was near Walden Pong. Over here, he cut his trees and built a house from scratch, using stones and sand from the forest while he got the windows, boards, and nails. The house he built was well within the budget of even a student. He believed that a person with more furniture in the house was poorer than someone with minimum items to his name.

In doing so, he showed that a person could live in their own way, avoiding the fate of people around them. Simply put, we do not need to conform to societal expectations, especially those who do not owe anything to us.

We can easily live a life of our own and rely on our innermost desires.

Many people incorrectly believe that living a simpler life/minimalism entail living a harsh life or accepting asceticism. There is extreme asceticism, which strives to go below minimalism. For example, when Prince Siddhartha Gautama first adopted asceticism, he ate only one grain of rice daily and had almost no flesh left on his bones. In this situation of extreme austerity, less is less, as it is a path to self-destruction. Siddhartha Gautama concluded that punishing the body would not result in enlightenment. So, before becoming the Buddha, he abandoned the austere lifestyle. The goal is the idea of "less is more." The focus is "more," "less" is the mean, and "more" is the end. In other words, the "more" you can gain from simpler life are: 1. more financial freedom, 2. less stress, 3. pursue your passion, 4. spend more time with your families and friends.

So, to live a life of minimalism, we must lead by example and begin to make conscious changes around us. You will need to make changes on personal and professional fronts here:

- Be prepared to say 'fuck you' to your boss and the company. It is the first step in stepping away from capitalism and living your own life. Leaving the capitalist rabbit hole means you no longer serve the system and its devious means.
- On the personal front, self-development can also be something to work on and develop. The more time you have for yourself, the better you can set to work on yourself.

A minimalist lifestyle takes a life of its own when applied comprehensively, changing the ballgame altogether.

Chapter 7
Common Sense Investing

Capitalism is the sum of its parts—capital and labor. When capital is absent, then the only sellable commodity is labor. Let me elaborate on that a bit.

Theoretically, capital will always oppress in a capitalism driven economy, while labor is oppressed as always. It has become an unwritten rule of thumb today.

In the previous chapters, we have talked about the necessity of living a simplistic life composed of these elements:
- Adopting a minimalistic lifestyle
- Saving money
- Steering clear of never-ending desires

These are the elements that help curtail the spiraling effects of capitalism. The more you adopt a simpler life, the less capitalism can oppress you since we cannot completely overthrow this system. The only solution is that we become more for-capital so we can benefit from the system. As you can see, this is related to the last few chapters. The more you save, the less materialistic you become, and the more capital you can accumulate.

When you have enough capital, you can utilize the best capital market in the world to accumulate money. This allows you to have your money produce money/passive income so that you do not have to work by providing your labor for money again. That is the price you have to pay to reach financial freedom.

Nevertheless, we all need to be very careful and mindful that the flaws of capitalism can get you again here. When it comes to investment, the concept of the simpler and better applies. The current financial institutions and Wall Street make the investment very complicated against it so that they can rip you off again.

This will only further prevent you from reaching financial and real freedom. In this case, even if you have enough capital, you still will not be able to benefit from the pros of capitalism effectively.

We all live a slow and linear life. That is why exponential effects are so difficult for us to grasp. This is most likely due to the shortness of our lives. As a result, to comprehend specific long-term and exponential ideas and their compounding effects, we must look at things from a much longer time horizon.

One of Indonesia's most beautiful and long-silent mountains, Tambora, exploded dramatically in 1815, killing 100,000 people with its detonation and accompanying tsunamis on the island of Sumbawa. With a scale 150 times greater than Mount St. Helens and an energy output equal to 60 000 Hiroshima-sized atom bombs, it was the largest volcanic eruption in the last 10,000 years. It took a long time for the news to spread back then. An anonymous letter from a merchant appeared in *The Times of London* seven months after the tragedy. However, Tambora's consequences had already begun to be felt. Sixty-six cubic miles of fine-grained smoke had accumulated in the stratosphere and blocked sunlight. This, in turn, caused the Earth's surface to become colder. However, Turner's famous sunsets were bleary-colored, and the Earth was engulfed in an oppressive, murky gloom that could not have been more depressing. Byron drew his inspiration for the above lines from the deathly stillness. 1816 was dubbed "the year without summer" because spring and summer never arrived. Crops failed to thrive across the board. Sixty-five thousand people perished in Ireland due to famine and a typhoid outbreak.

Even at the turn of the 19th century, the climate had already begun to sour. In Europe and North America, a Little Ice Age, as it has come to be known, allowed for all kinds of winter festivities, such as ice-skating races on the canals of the Netherlands, that is now essentially impossible. In other words, it was a time when people's thoughts were occupied with the subject of frigidity. This suggests that nineteenth-century geologists may have been naive about how much of their surroundings had been formed by glaciers and cold that would have destroyed even the most lavish of fairs.

The scientists were aware that the past possessed some peculiar qualities. The terrain of Europe was strewn with unexplainable oddities, such as the bones of frigid reindeer in the mild south of France and enormous rocks stranded in unlikely places. They frequently came up with creative but not particularly logical explanations for these occurrences. When attempting to explain how granite boulders came to rest high up on the limestone flanks of the Jura Mountains, a French naturalist by the name of de Luc hypothesized that perhaps they had been fired, thereby compressing air in caves, like how corks come out of a popgun. Erratic is the phrase used to describe a boulder that has moved from its original location; nevertheless, during the nineteenth century, the term seems to be used more frequently to refer to hypotheses than to rocks.

However, the local peasants, untainted by scientific dogma, had a greater understanding of the situation. Jean de Charpentier, a naturalist, once related the story of how, in 1834, he was strolling down a country path with a Swiss woodcutter when the two began discussing the rocks along the roadside. The woodcutter explained to him that the stones originated from the Grimsel, a granite zone located some distance away. " When asked how he felt these stones had gotten to their current location, he answered my question without hesitation by saying, " Because the glacier-covered as far as the town of Bern a long time ago. "

Charpentier was happy. He had arrived at the same conclusion on his own, but it was shot down whenever he brought up the concept in scientific settings. Another Swiss naturalist named Louis Agassiz was one of Charpentier's closest friends. After some initial skepticism, Agassiz soon came to embrace the thesis, and by the end, he had almost wholly appropriated it as his own.

Agassiz had already completed his education in Paris under the tutelage of Cuvier, and he was subsequently appointed to the position of Professor of Natural History at the College of Neuchatel in Switzerland. In 1837, a botanist named Karl Schimper, a friend of Agassiz's was the first person to create the term "ice age." He also proposed that there was good evidence to show that ice had once lain heavily across not only the Swiss Alps but also over much of Europe, Asia, and North America. It was a revolutionary idea. He gave Agassiz his notes, which he later came to regret as Agassiz later claimed it was his idea deeply. Agassiz got the credit for what Schimper felt was his theory.

In any case, Agassiz was successful in making the field his own. Agassiz was unfazed by the opposition and persistently traveled to promote his theory. In 1840, he presented a paper at a conference of the British Association for the Advancement of Science held in Glasgow. During this meeting, the famous Charles Lyell chastised him for his work. Next year, the Geological Society of Edinburgh passed a resolution admitting that the theory might have some general merit but that there was no way that any of it related to Scotland. The decision also stated that the idea might have some general merit.

In the 1860s, journals and other scholarly periodicals in Britain started getting writings on hydrostatics, electricity, and other scientific topics from a professor at Anderson's University in Glasgow named James Croll. One of the papers that discussed how changes in the Earth's orbit might have led to ice ages was published in 1864. It was immediately acknowledged as a work of the highest caliber when it was first presented to the scientific community. When it was finally revealed that Croll was not a university professor but a janitor, it came with many surprises and possibly even a little bit of an embarrassment.

Croll was the first person to propose that cyclical changes in the shape of the Earth's orbit, from elliptical to nearly circular to elliptical again, might explain the beginning and end of ice ages. These orbital changes are similar to how a pendulum swing back and forth. Before this discovery, nobody had ever contemplated the possibility that changes in Earth's climate could have an astronomical basis. People in Britain started to show more openness to the idea that at one point in Earth's history, some regions were covered in ice, and practically all of this openness can be attributed to the appealing explanation that Croll put up. Croll got a job at the Geological Survey of Scotland and was widely honored when his inventiveness and aptitude were recognized.

On the other hand, his ideas quickly became outdated, which is something that does occur. Less than a decade after his passing, his successor in the chair of geology at Harvard said that the "so-called glacial period... so popular a few years ago among glacial geologists may now be rejected without hesitation." This statement was made about the glacier geologists. In the early

1900s, a Serbian mechanical engineer named Milutin Milankovitch became interested in celestial motions. Milankovitch concluded Croll's idea was too simplistic, not wrong.

As Earth moves through space, its tilt, pitch, and wobble alter the length and intensity of sunlight falling on any piece of land. Its obliquity, precession, and eccentricity change over time. Milankovitch questioned if these complicated cycles were related to ice ages. The cycles' varied lengths—approximately 20,000, 40,000, and 100,000 years, but ranging by a few thousand years—made pinpointing their junction sites over lengthy periods problematic. Milankovitch had to calculate the angle and duration of solar radiation at every latitude and season for a million years.

In 1930 Milankovitch was proven correct that ice ages and planetary wobble are related, but he assumed a steady increase in harsh winters caused them. Wladimir Köppen perceived the process as more nuanced and unsettling.

Köppen concluded that cool summers, not harsh winters, produced ice ages. If summers are not hot enough for the ice to melt, the reflecting surface bounces back more sunlight, worsening the chilling effect and encouraging further snowfall. Self-perpetuating results are likely. As snow turned into ice, the location grew cooler, causing more ice to form. "It's not the volume of snow that generates ice sheets, but that it lasts," says glaciologist Gwen Schultz. Unseasonable summers may trigger an ice age. Leftover snow reflects heat and increases cooling. Once the ice starts expanding, it moves, explains McPhee. Ice age and rising glaciers.

The most important thing learned from the ice ages is that extraordinary outcomes can be achieved without applying striking force. If something compounds, or if a small amount of growth acts as the fuel for further development, then a modest beginning point might lead to results that are so spectacular that they appear to defy logic. It is conceivable for it to defy logic to such an extent that you end up underestimating what is possible, where growth originates, and where it can lead.

When we deal with money, the case is precisely the same. When you invest in it, you need to keep two aspects in mind: the return and the cost. First, let's pay attention to the return on investment, then analyze the cost.

Since 1928, the average annual return on the U.S. stock market has been 9.8 percent. Approximately every three out of every four years, the market goes up. There has not been a single 20-year stretch during which the United States stock market experienced a nominal decline. Over the years, I have reviewed statistics of this kind to the point of exhaustion.

The question is, why does this happen? Why, over time, does the stock market continue to go up? I am aware that many people believe that the Illuminati is in control of the stock market or low-interest rates; however, others believe that the Federal Reserve controls these things. The expansion of the economy and the increase in profits of corporations are the primary factors behind the stock market's rise over time.

Earnings per share for the companies included in the S&P 500 were $1.11 in 1928, while dividends paid out by companies were $0.78 per share. At the time, it was impossible to do so; nonetheless, if you had been able to hold an index fund, those would have been the cash flows you would have received per share at the time.

In 2021, the figures will have increased to $197.87 and $60.40. This indicates that earnings on the United States stock market have grown at an annual pace of 6% over the past 94 years, while dividends have increased at an annual rate of 5% during the same period.

If you invest in the stock market, you will have the opportunity to share in the earnings and cash flows of the companies you have invested in. You have the chance to profit from their creativity, investment, and expansion. As an illustration, let's look at the stock with the most market value.

Apple's revenue by the end of 2014 was more than 182 billion dollars, and the company made a net profit of 39.5 billion dollars. Apple's sales for the fiscal year that ended in 2021 were

$386 billion, while the business made a net profit of $94.7 billion during that same period.

The company's earnings increased by more than 140 percent, while its sales increased by more than double. At the same time, Apple distributed more than 103 billion dollars in dividends to its stockholders. In addition, Apple is not the only company that gives dividends to its stockholders.

Even though this number has decreased over the past several decades due to the surge in share buybacks, the average payout ratio for S&P 500 businesses since 1928 has been more excellent than 50 percent. This indicates that corporations have distributed more than half their profits in cold hard cash to their shareholders.

In 1982, the stock market's total value in the United States was estimated to be $1.2 trillion. The current value of Apple by itself is more significant than $2.5 trillion. The rise in the stock market can be attributed to the fact that firms continue to expand and become more profitable over time.

If you hold stocks, you get a percentage of the growth that the company experiences. Even if there are occasions when it goes down in the short term, the stock market generally moves higher over the long run. When you stop considering it, the stock market will inevitably go down. If you didn't occasionally have your face ripped off, it wouldn't be able to deliver the kind of lucrative returns. If $10,000 had been invested in the United States stock market in 1928, it would have grown to around $66 million by today's standards.

If you see this trend above, it can help you focus on long term and compound reinvesting. Instead of being afraid of market volatility, see it as the best friend of investing. If you can consistently apply the concept of dollar cost averaging, you will be able to harness the volatility to its fullest. Let's look at another example.

The story of how Warren Buffett accumulated his money has been the subject of many publications. Many of them are excellent. But very few people pay enough attention to the most apparent reality: Buffett's riches aren't just the result of him being a good investor; instead, it's the result of him being a successful investor ever since he was a youngster. Warren Buffett's net worth was approximately $98 billion when this chapter was written. Out of that total, $84.2 billion was amassed by him after he became 50 years old. When he was in his mid-60s and had already qualified for Social Security, he received $81.5 billion. The legendary investor Warren Buffett is a terrific businessman. If you attribute all his success to his investment ability, you are missing an important factor. The true secret to his success is that he has been a terrific investment for the better part of three-quarters of a century. If he had begun investing when he was in his 30s and retired when he was in his 60s, not many people would have known his name.

Consider the following thought experiment to be conducted. Buffett made his first significant investment when he was only ten years old. At 30, he already had a net worth of one million dollars, equivalent to $9.3 million when adjusted for inflation. What if he was a more average guy who spent his teens and 20s traveling the world and discovering what he was genuinely passionate about, and by the time he was 30 years old, his net worth was, for example, $25,000?

And let's imagine he went on to earn the fantastic annual investment returns he's been able to create (22 percent annually), but he stopped investing when he was 60 years old so he could play golf and spend time with his grandchildren instead of continuing to invest. What is a reasonable approximation of the current value of his estate? Not even close to $84.5 billion. $11.9 million. A reduction of 99.9 percent compared to his actual net worth. It is possible to attribute virtually all of Warren Buffett's financial success to the fact that he established a solid financial foundation when he was younger and maintained a healthy level of longevity when he was older. His expertise is in finance, but time is key to his success. This is how the process of compounding works.

We have assessed common sense investing from the perspective of compounding return. However, the cost of investing is even more critical for ordinary people. From a long-term perspective, compounding returns can help you achieve financial freedom, but compounding costs, expensive costs, can take away your freedom and wealth. Now, let's examine the situation.

All financial institutions want to encourage you through tactfully marketing to invest your money into mutual funds. Even worse, the managed portfolios consisted of dozens of mutual funds. According to research and studies, 96% of actively managed mutual funds do not beat the market. Yet they charge you a crazy amount.

Let's make some simplified analysis: say each mutual fund charges you 1% fees (this is an underestimate), and managed portfolio can charge you 1.5% advisory fees (that is, to have the financial institution and financial advisors give you advice. We will figure out what kind of advice they give you.) on top of there. With all other fees, conservatively speaking, you can quickly pay at least 3% or more fees. 3%! This is a big rip-off. Usually, your investment portfolios are your long-term money. Considering the power of compounding, this annual 3% fee can inflict massive damage on you over time. So, once again, when you intend to let your money work for you to help you be financially free, you are ripped off big time by the evil part of capitalism again. On the other hand, you can invest your money into a low-cost ETF that can allow you to access entire S&P 500 stocks at only 0.03%, which is nearly 0.

Let's do some calculations. Suppose Mike, Kevin and Linda are all 30 years old and invested $500k (I purposely make a big amount to emphasize the astonishment of cost over the long term) for 35 years. Assume that the gross annual return is 8%. Mike invests in a 3% fee managed account. After 35 years, his $500k will become $2,866,859. Kevin's investment cost is 1.5%. His $500k will become $4,834,189. Linda invests in a 0.03% low-cost ETF or a portfolio of ETFs. Her $500k will become $8,061,746 or $8 million! Do you see the huge difference between Mike and Linda? We are looking at $2.86 million vs. $8 million here. Even a 1.5% difference in fees between Mike and Kevin still creates a $2 million gap after 35 years. If you think this is NOT a big rip-off from capitalism—financial institutions or Wall Street—what else is?

Based on this alone, you should all fire your financial advisors. Everyone can be their financial advisor by simply doing some basic studies. I had been a financial advisor, so I knew what it was like. You pay 1.5% advisory fees and 1% expense for mutual funds. Most of the time, when markets are down, when you call your advisors, or when you do an annual review, they usually tell you this: Don't worry. Focus on your long-term goal. Markets will go back up. Keep your money invested. No need to worry about short-term volatility. You are still on track to meeting your financial goals...."

Most of their sales pitch is along these lines. Whatever they say is not incorrect, but do you think it is worth it for you to pay so many fees? In terms of absolute amount, it is $5.2 million. That will cost you ($8 million - $2.8 million). You can read the following two chapters or buy a few good investment books to help you become your financial advisor. You will understand 80% of the message most financial advisors would provide. Many people like to save money on repairing their houses, so they learn to become handymen. Isn't it worth spending a little time and money to acquire this skill?

I call it the psychology of investing—buy and hold, dollar cost averaging, and focus on the long term. This introductory psychology of investing saves you around $5 million over time. No brainer. Please do not take my word for it. Look at what John C. Bogle, the founder of Vanguard and the author of *The Little Book of Common Sense Investing* has strongly encouraged people should only invest in low-cost index funds. He said, "The index fund eliminates the risks of individual stocks, market sectors, and manager selection. Only stock market risk remains." He also mentioned that when you understand how our financial markets work, you will see that an index fund is the only investment that guarantees that you will capture your fair share of a business's returns.

Thanks to the miracle of compounding, the wealth accumulations generated by those returns over the years have been little short of fantastic." This statement is in line with the astonishing calculation we showed above regarding how compound power can make a massive difference over time on different costs. Let me use one more statement by John Bogle to summarize my message: "Before deducting the cost of investing, beating the stock market is a zero-sum game. In the game of investing, the financial institutions/croupiers always win, and investors as a group lose.

After deducting the cost of investing, beating the stock market is a loser's game. Less to Wall Street croupiers means more to Main Street investors." In the next chapter—Chapter 8—I will talk about the fundamental characteristic of investing, finance, and business based on the theory of simpler the better or common sense, allowing everyone to be their financial advisors and fund managers. There is no need to let the financial croupiers of capitalism rip you off anymore.

In *Commons Sense Investing*, John Bogle also uses Charles T Munger's message on this issue. Mr. Munger puts it this way: "The general money management systems require people to pretend to do something they can't do and like something they don't. It is a funny business because, on a net basis, the whole investment management business gives no value added to all buyers combined. That's the way it must work. Mutual funds usually charge 2% per year. Worse, the brokers switch people between funds, costing another three to four percent. So, inevitably, the public is getting a terrible product from the professionals. I think it is disgusting. It is much better to be part of a system that delivers value to the people who buy the product."

Here is how the *Economist* of London puts it: "The truth is that, for the most part, fund managers have offered extremely poor value for money. Stretches of underperformance almost always follow their records of outperformance. Over long periods, hardly any fund managers have beaten the market average. And all the while, they charge big fees from their clients for promising the privilege of losing their money."

Therefore, in conclusion, by adopting a simpler, better lifestyle, we can reduce or minimize the oppression from capitalism. By adopting common sense and simpler, the better investment style, we can also prevent Wall Street—the core of our capitalism—from ripping us off.

Chapter 8

The Psychology of Investing

Let me reiterate this. Suppose you want to effectively invest your money to earn a fair return and make your money work for you as hard as possible. In that case, you need to do two things immediately: fire your fund managers and financial advisors!!!! Let me repeat this message 1000 times............. The success of investing for ordinary people like you and me relies on common sense and the psychology of investing. That is something you should spend time learning and harnessing. And this is not difficult for you to learn and harness. In this chapter, let me try to review some analyses for you.

Wall Street crooks purposely complicate finance and investment so they can use their sheer sales force and marketing craftmanship to legally steal your hard-earned money from you. Investment should be straightforward. There are only two main categories of asset classes: equity/stock and debt/bonds. Equity can be divided into subcategories: large-cap, mid-cap, small-cap, developed markets (such as Europe and Japan), and emerging markets (such as China, India, Brazil, etc.). Debts/bonds can be divided into Treasury bonds, Investment grade bonds, corporate bonds, Municipal bonds, Junk bonds, international bonds, etc.

Compounding power is the first thing you must consider for common sense investing. Let time be your best friend. Let's say a young person who is 22 years old invest $10,000 into the stock market for 43 years at age 65 to retire at an annual return of 10%.

By the end of 43 years, he will have $602,401. If this person is 32 years old, they only have 33 years to invest; at age 65, the money will be $232,252. So let time be your best friend. However, if the annual return is 15%, after 43 years, you will have $4,073,870. You are in pretty good shape. So, there is why Albert Eisenstein says the most powerful force in the universe is compound interest. The most famous investor Warren Buffet has been achieving around a 20% average return per year. So if you can earn 20% per year, your $10k after 43 years will become $25million. That is nice. However, if you want to achieve 20% per year, you must invest in high-risk investments.

Let's say you invest in a high-risk asset, the average return is still 20%, but every 12 years, your investment will suffer a 50% loss; by the end, you will only end up approximately with $1.8 million instead of $25 million. Do you see a vast difference? So, the critical element here is to avoid any significant loss. Warren Buffet's golden rule # 1 is Never to Lose money. Rule # 2 is Never forget Rule # 1. So how not lose money?

Let me clarify stock market volatility is not losing money. If today's market is down tomorrow up, that is not the definition of losing money. It would help if you didn't focus on daily stock market volatility. Instead, it is the probability of losing your capital permanently. So, I would not invest in start-ups and small companies but in large, mature, and well-established ones. In other words, we need to invest in something you can understand, such as Coke, McDonald's, and Wal-Mart.

This is an essential element of the psychology of investing. People tend to buy high and sell low. The most important thing you need to learn as a long-term investor is to manage to stomach the market's volatility. When you invest in the companies mentioned above when your portfolio is down a lot, you can keep reminding yourself: I am investing in Coke, McDonald's, Starbucks, and Wal-Mart; people are using these companies every day; they are everywhere; they are not going down, they are the backbone of US economy and the USA as a country is not going down, Warren Buffet said never bet against the USA, they will come back......etc."

See, you don't need a financial advisor to tell you the message above; all you need is to invest in things you understand to manage the psychology of investing. If you invest in small companies and emerging countries' stocks, when they drop a lot, it will be more difficult for you to manage the psychology of investing since you don't even know what companies you are investing in. This is how Wall Street crooks get you. They tactfully put different stocks and bonds into so call package products, making them very complicated to understand.

The fund managers can hire their delicate sales forces- financial advisors- to use beautiful language to get you into something that would cost you 3-4% per year regardless of you make money or lose money. In this case, since you feel that you don't understand any of these package products because they convince you investment and finance are as complicated as rocky science, you can't do it on your own; you need to rely on experts entirely. In other words, you are the ones who provide all the money, assuming all the risks, but they can make guaranteed money. Financial advisors are more of sales and marketing people than someone who provides invaluable expertise. They will do anything to convince you to leave your money in package products as long as possible. So they can keep collecting fees from you.

Another reason is that we have already mentioned you should let time be your best friend by using the compounding power. So you don't need to take a high risk to chase inconsistent returns as in the demonstration we showed above. Warren Buffet's rule of investment is never to lose money. So average historical returns for these large companies are sufficient for us to reach long-term financial goals.

Let me kind of list out a few critical factors when you consider what type of companies you should invest in: 1. Invest in large and well-established companies, 2 Understand how the company makes money, 3, High barriers to enter (wide moats), 4, fewer debts, 5, immune to extrinsic factors (for example consumer staple companies like Coke, Wal Mart, no matter what happen to the economy people have to use their products and services) 6, Invest at a reasonable price (that is why you should let market volatility be your best friends and do dollar-cost averaging, if markets don't go down, you will hardly have chance to buy at a reasonable price), 7, invest in a company that can last forever. A few good examples to meet these seven factors can be Coca-Cola, Wal-Mart, Costco, Philip Morris, etc.

We, ordinary people, don't even need to understand Warren Buffet's picking stock skills. Nor do we need to bother exactly which large company stock we should invest in; even a company like Coca-Cola, which meets all the above conditions, may still face problems in the future; there is no guarantee. So it can always be easy to invest in low-cost index funds or ETFs in the entire market (remember, various studies show that 85%-96% percent of fund managers can't beat the market over time but charge 3-4% fees). For example, if you want to invest in Coca-Cola, Wal-Mart, a consumer staple, or defensive stock, you can invest in XLP - Consumer Staples Select Sectors. Let's see what the top ten stocks it holds are:

Holdings	% Portfolio Weight	P/E	Economic Moat
Procter & Gamble Co	15.67	24.69	Wide
Coca-Cola Co	10.79	26.11	Wide
PepsiCo Inc	10.14	25.64	Wide
Costco Wholesale Corp	9.27	33.90	Wide
Philip Morris International Inc	4.93	18.05	Wide
Mondelez International Inc Class A	4.64	22.32	Wide
Walmart Inc	4.40	21.83	Wide
Altria Group Inc	4.38	10.82	Wide
Colgate-Palmolive Co	3.32	25.32	Wide
The Estee Lauder	2.73	27.25	Wide

Companies Inc Class A

As you can see on the above chart, these are the top 10 holdings of this ETF, such as P & G, Coca-Cola, Pepsi, Costco, etc. Under PE ratio, you can see the PE ratio for each stock (the lower the PE ratio, the more reasonable the value is); also, under economics moat, you can see Wide for all these companies. That is our condition #3, High Barrier of entry. In other words, invest in XLP. You can access these best consumer staple companies in the US or even the world since these are all global companies. The fees or expense ratio of XLP is only 0.1% compared to the 3-4% that you have to pay to your fund manager and advisors.

Most importantly, when markets are down, you can look at your holding and quickly remind yourself: I am investing in Coca-Cola, Pepsi, Costco, Colgate, Wal Mart; these companies won't go under; they will come back. That way, it is improbable for you to freak out and sell at the low. Another characteristic of the consumer staple or defensive sector is, just like its name, its stock prices are relatively more stable and defensive. When there are bull markets, its return is likely to underperform compared to those sectors, such as technology and consumer discretionary. However, when the markets are bad, their performance will likely to be better. For example, as of this writing, on May 13, 2022, this year, the stock market is doing poorly due to high inflation.

While S&P 500 (SPY OR VOO) is down 17%, the technology sector (XLK) is down 24%, consumer discretionary (XLY) is down 28%, and XLP consumer staple is ONLY down 1.24%; this is a fantastic performance when the overall market is down so much. For those who want consistent and staple returns but don't want to stomach too much market volatility, this is an excellent choice of low-cost ETF. Remember Warren Buffett's rule never loses money. Think about this, let's say you invest $10,000 in technology XLK, you are down 20% on year 1, and you will only have $8k, to begin with at the very beginning of year 2; how much return do you need to make on year 2 to get back to $10k? Not 20% but 25%. If you lose 50% in the first year, you need 100% to return to your principal in year 2.

This is just simple math. However, if you lose only 5% in the first year, you only need to make 5.2% to return to your principal. That is also why you need to do dollar-cost averaging. Take advantage when markets are down since no one can predict the markets. Some people may feel these large consumer defensive companies are boring, which would not provide a good return over time. But XLP provided an average annual return of 10.08% in the last 15 years, 11.44% last ten years, 9.90% for five years, 13.3% for three years, and 11.64% for one year. Though past performance can't guarantee future performance, at least we can see a pattern from history: consistency.

In the last 15 years, an average of 10% per year is excellent. It included the 2008 financial crisis in which XLP was down 14.97% while S&P 500 was down about 37%. That shows the defensive characteristics of consumer staple stocks. Now, hold your breath. Let's look at some numbers again. If you invested $100k into XLP 15 years ago, it would become $445,390 today, which is not bad. But how much would you have now if you save money, live a simpler life, and put $2000 a month into XLP for the last 15 years? The answer is $1,281,240. If you can do $3000 a month, it would be $1.7 million, and if you can do $5000 a month, it will be $2.5 million, and so on.

If we extend the time to 30 years, let's say you invest $3000 a month into XLP on a 10% annual return, $100k will become $8.8 million !!!!!! If $5000 a month for 30 years, it will be $13 million !!!!!!!! But if you have to pay Wall Street 3% per year, your $13 million will be reduced to $7 million. Therefore, all the chapters are connected. The simpler lifestyle you live, you follow common sense investment, not letting Wall Street gets you again on expensive fees.

While it is not difficult to stomach a 1% drop on XLP, what if this year you invest in XLY consumer discretionary, which as of this writing, is down 28%? What should I do? It is called consumer discretionary because people do not have to consume their products and services when the economy is bad, inflation is high, which is why it is more vulnerable to external conditions. So, in bull markets, it should provide higher returns than XLP. But once again, let's look at its holding.

Holdings	% Portfolio Weight	P/E	Economic Moat
Amazon.com Inc	19.03	39.84	Wide
Tesla Inc	18.65	60.98	Narrow
McDonald's Corp	5.96	24.69	Wide
The Home Depot Inc	5.44	18.08	Wide
Nike Inc Class B	4.50	23.64	Wide
Lowe's Companies Inc	4.22	14.37	Wide
Target Corp	3.40	14.88	None
Booking Holdings Inc	2.75	23.31	Narrow
Starbucks Corp	2.62	22.78	Wide

TJX Companies Inc		2.18	17.51 Narrow

As you can see, you are investing in companies like Amazon, Tesla, McDonald's, Home Depot, Nike, Target, etc. Though your money is down 28%, you can once again remind yourself: I am investing in these reputable companies; they are the backbone of the US economy, don't bet against the US; they will come back. They are great companies; when they are down, it is a good chance for me to do dollar-cost averaging to keep investing the money I save every month, etc. The most important thing to be your fund manager and financial advisor is transparency; in other words, you need to know and understand what you are investing in.

    Those Wall Street crooks don't want you to have a lot of transparency. On top of these large-cap funds, put your money into the mid-cap, small-cap, developed market (non-US), emerging markets, commodity, junk bonds, security back mortgage, etc. They want you to invest in many things that you don't understand. So, when markets are down so much, when you panic, you can only or mainly rely on financial advisors and these financial firms to tell you: don't worry, it will come back over and over again. So basically, you are paying them crazy fees over time to have them tell you something you could have said yourself, if, only if, you invest in something you understand.

It is not easy to overcome fear but more difficult to overcome greed. When your portfolio is down, you have no choice but to leave it and wait for the money to come back. But when the market is hot, it is not easy for you to stick with your financial plan, not chase hot stocks, and not buy high. Let me use another example. In January 2019, two good friends, John and Peter, invested $100k into XLP and famous high-tech small and midsize stocks ETF ARKK, respectively.

For the next three and half years (as of this writing on May 13, 2022, XLP's annual returns are: 27.43% for 2019, 10.15% for
2020, 17.20% for 2021, and as of May 13, 2022, YTD return is 1.24%. ARKK's returns are: 35.58% on 2019, 156.91% on 2020, -23.38% on 2021 and as of May 13, 2022, YTD -58.78%. So don't get me wrong, I am not saying which investment is better. I am simply using these two ETFs as an example to demonstrate the greed of investing. By the end of 2020, John's $100k invested in XLP would become approximately $140k, which is a great return, two years of 40% return. However, Peter's $100k invested in ARKK would become approximately $348k !!!!!

Everyone closes their eyes, puts themselves into John's situation, and imagines if you were John, what would you do? At first, you saw your money grow from $100k to $140k; would you be happy? Of course, you would. However, when Peter told you his $100k has become $348K, how would you feel again? You would probably feel like shit. What would you likely do subsequently? Most people would fail to overcome the feeling of greed and switch their Investment from XLP to ARKK. Well, if John switched his $140k into ARKK on January 2, 2021, his money would have become $44,215 by May 13, 2022; ouch, that hurts. However, if John sticks with XLP, his $140k would have become approximately $162k.

Assuming Peter has held ARKK till today, May 13, 2022, he will end up with about $109k. Let me put them together one more time. If John and Peter had stuck with XLP and ARKK for the last three and half years, by the end of the second year, John and Peter would have $140k and $348k, respectively. By May 13, 2022, John and Peter would have ended up with $162k and $109k, respectively. Do you see the message I want to deliver here? Once again, mathematically, it asserts Warren Buffet's rule again: Never Lose Money.

Well, I am not saying ARKK is bad; probably, after 1015 years, it would have a higher return than XLP; no one knows. I am just saying to manage the psychology of money to find ways to overcome greed is more important. When bull markets return when you are under pressure to chase higher returns, please remind yourself of this lesson again. Focus on your financial goal and remind yourself that you don't need to chase a higher and riskier return to reach your financial goals. Consistent and stable return, under the power of compounding, will still serve your cause. Be patient and disciplined. Also, keep in mind that not all ETFs are passively managed funds. In this case, ARKK is an actively managed fund by Cathie Wood and her team. Therefore, ARKK's fee is 0.75%, while XLP's is 0.1%. Let's look at the top 10 holding of ARKK.

Holdings	% Portfolio Weight	P/E	Economic Moat
Tesla Inc	9.30	64.52	Narrow
Roku Inc Class A	8.36	-133.33	None
Zoom Video Communications Inc	8.09	26.81	Narrow
Exact Sciences Corp	5.77	-11.81	None
Block Inc Class A	5.44	104.17	Narrow
Teladoc Health Inc	4.92	-1.52	None
Twilio Inc Class A	4.37	-196.08	Narrow
UiPath Inc Class A	4.10	-1,111.11	—
CRISPR Therapeutics AG	4.07	-6.09	None
Coinbase Global Inc Ordinary Shares - Class A	3.92	-7.99	None

Many of these companies are either mid-size or small size without making any profits. However, as Cathie Wood strongly suggests, many of them can potentially become new FAANG stocks in the long term. However, according to my seven factors of selecting stocks, most of them are not large and well-established firms. Most importantly, on factor #3, the higher entry barrier, none of these companies have a wide moat. So, if you want consistent and stable return using the power of compounding, this probably is not a good fit for you. Also, many of us do not fully understand how these companies make money because they are not making any money yet. But it wouldn't hurt if you invest a small percentage of your asset into ARKK and let it ride like a rollercoaster for longer-term money.

    Each sector of stocks performs differently under different economic conditions. For example, when the economy and markets are not good, such as so far this year 2022, defensive sectors, such as consumer staples, utility, and health care, should perform better. Consumer discretionary/cyclical sectors tend to do well when the economic condition is better. The gold and oil & gas sectors tend to do well when inflation is high. When interest is higher financial industry tends to do well. Eleven sectors consist of the entire S&P 500 index. Let me list them along with relevant ETFs that can allow you to access them: 1. Energy, XLE, 2. Materials, XLB, 3. Industrials, XLI, 4 Utilities, XLU. 5 Healthcare, XLV, 6 Financials, XLF. 7 Consumer Discretionary, XLY, 8 Consumer staple, XLP, 9 Information Technology, XLK, 10 Communication XLC, 11 real estates or REIT, XLRE.

    Even though we know in theory and in general how each sector reacts under various economic conditions, there is merely anyone who can consistently and successfully predict the markets and rotate between industries, especially ordinary people like you and me. If financial advisors tell you the fund managers can beat the market, at least according to statistics, 85-96% of the time, they are wrong. So, another alternative is you can invest in the S&P 500 index, such as SPY or VOO; both have meager costs and consist of all 11 sectors mentioned above.

Take Warren Buffett's advice to ordinary people; he said we should all put money into S&P 500 index fund. At least in the last decade, his portfolio underperformed S&P. This is also a great way to discipline your psychology of investing. When the market tanks, such as so far this year, SPY is down 15%. In this case, I can keep reminding myself: I am investing in the best 500 companies in the US or even the world. Don't bet against America; they will exist and come back. People are using these 500 companies' products and services every day. I should see the market downturn, my best friend, to dollar-cost averaging into the ETF......etc." Since SPY already diversifies your money into 500 companies across 11 sectors, how would you feel not safe about your investment? Let's look at the portfolio of SPY:

Holdings	% Portfolio Weight	P/E	Economic Moat
Apple Inc	6.70	24.15	Narrow
Microsoft Corp	5.75	24.21	Wide
Amazon.com Inc	2.91	42.02	Wide
Alphabet Inc Class A	2.05	20.41	Wide
Alphabet Inc Class C	1.90	20.49	Wide
Tesla Inc	1.89	64.52	Narrow
Berkshire	1.67	23.15	Wide

Hathaway Inc Class B			
Johnson & Johnson	1.37	17.24	Wide
Meta Platforms Inc Class A	1.35	16.50	Wide
UnitedHealth Group Inc	1.34	22.47	Narrow

Once again when your SPY or VOO goes down quite a bit. You can look at this transparent holding and remind yourself: I am investing in Apple, Microsoft, Amazon, Google, Johnson & Johnson, Berkshire Hathaway (Warren Buffet's company), and United Health Care; I will be fine; they will come back, I need to buy more when they are down."

See, I hope I have demonstrated how you can become your fund managers and financial advisors above with few efforts to harness this skill by yourself. You don't need to invest in something you don't understand, which is a very wrong way of investing your hard earn money to achieve your financial freedom. Even though you may not know how all these 500 companies make money, at least you know they collectively represent the most significant portion of the US economy.

If the USA as a country will not go down, these 500 companies will not go down; though some companies may fail and disappear over time, you don't need to win all to win. When you approach a financial institution and an advisor, they will likely convince you to put your money into BROADLY diversified managed funds. That will include a combination of most subsectors of stocks and bonds, such as large-cap, mid-cap, small-cap, international stocks, treasury bonds, investment-grade bonds, Muni bonds, junk bonds, etc.

Now, think about this let's say you invest into a balanced portfolio of a managed account, which includes either 50% equity and 50% bond, or 60/40 something. Historically and realistically, a broadly diversified balanced portfolio should only give you around 5% gross return. However, your overall fees don't change much, though some bond funds have a lower expense, which should still be about 3%. How does it make sense? What kind of business is this? You provide all the money, bear all the risks, and you can only potentially, not guarantee, a 5% gross return.

In comparison, the financial institutions are guaranteed to earn 3% annually whether they make you money or lose you money? Does it make sense? Look, many of these financial advisors make middle and high six-digit income or even seven-digit income. They are making more than top doctors. I am not saying they do not provide any value, but do you think they have made valuable contributions to your investment in proportion to their income?

Their high incomes come at your expense. Assuming you don't call them daily, they will probably meet you once or twice a year for a financial review, all at the most, once a quarter. What they will do during the review is reiterate that you should focus on long-term investment, buy and hold, and don't panic about market volatility. Review your financial goals; if there is any change, they will reallocate your money accordingly. All these are good and necessary but is it worth you to pay them that much for that kind of work.

If you have $100k invested in the managed portfolio compared to if you have $1 million, the amount of time and work they spend on you is pretty much the same. Say for $100k; you pay them $3000 per year, and for $1 million, you pay $30k. Even if you hire a lawyer to do legal work for you, they need to do ten times more work to charge you ten times more money. But financial advisors do pretty much the same amount of work.

Once again, if you invest in large, reputable, well-established companies and understand how these companies make money, you invest your money in low-cost ETF and Index funds, you can already beat at least 85% of fund managers over time. You can be your financial advisor to console yourself that you need to focus on the long term; these stocks will come back; you should buy more when prices are low." That can save you an unimaginable amount of money, helping you use your cash to reach the dream of financial freedom.

Chapter 9
The All-Weather Portfolio

Among several things, a financial advisor will tell you to be smart about your investments. To this end, they will suggest placing your money into a diversified balanced/moderate portfolio consisting of fifty percent of stocks and the remainder fifty percent in bonds. This becomes a sixty-forty or forty-sixty ratio, or maybe a fifty-fifty percent ratio. This division aims to spread your investment widely into several areas (called financial products). These financial products are mostly funds, which consist of only two categories for the most part:

Bonds

Stocks

Many of these funds are the same and rarely diversify each other. As I have mentioned in the last chapter, financial institutions are just there for profiteering and abusing consumer ignorance. They reduce the funds' transparency and then provide never-ending justifications for all these additional charges and invisible fees.

However, the million-dollar question is: Do these balanced funds diversify and spread the risk as promised?

Ray Dalio thinks differently about this. The founder and co-chief investment officer of the world's-biggest hedge fund—Bridgewater Associates—says that ninety-five percent of the risk lies in stocks. The hedge fund giant opines that those stocks are more volatile than bonds, which is true. As we know, stocks are thrice more volatile than conventional bonds. So, the risk is hardly lowered when we equally divide our investment between stocks and bonds. The stocks still have that same ninety-five percent (95%) risk in that case as well.

What does that tell you overall? The risk is not lowered here because the investor will still bear the brunt of this risk when the market underperforms.

So, here, let us take an instance. From 1970 to 2022, S&P 500 has lost eleven (11) times in forty-two years. Thus, the cumulative losses stand over a hundred and sixty-three. The bonds did a bit well during this time, losing only five times (5) in forty-two (42) years. Also, the cumulative losses were only seven and a half percent (7.5%).

Ideally, if the portfolio is evenly divided at fifty-fifty percent (50/50), the stocks will still incur a loss of ninety-five percent (95%) even then. The consensus is that when the stocks rise, the bonds will decline and vice versa to curtail this risk. But that does not really matter much on the market. The heightened fees are still there, which also defeats the investment purpose. Ray Dalio explains it like this:

"When you look at most portfolios, they have a very strong bias to do well in good times and bad in bad times." Therefore, what kind of diversification is it when the risk is hardly curtailed? This is something that financial advisors will not tell you for several reasons.

So, over here, I will introduce the unconventional all-weather portfolio by Ray Dalio. It is also known as an all-season portfolio, which implies that it works for any/all economic climates. However, its trump card drives down the risk and maximizes the returns. Anyone can do this. You must select five low-cost ETFs and avoid a financial advisor's three percent annual fees. This same financial advisor will largely be unable to accomplish this scale of risk-reward results that this portfolio is capable of, which says a lot about these financial mavericks.

The risk-reward ratio is a concept closely connected with any investment option. People deploy standard deviation in order to measure the extent of volatility, which helps identify the risk. The higher the standard deviation (SD), the higher the risk/volatility.

Let us consider two investment portfolios named A and B. Portfolio A has a ten-percent return (10%), whereas portfolio B has a return of nine percent (9%).

Which one is better?

There is no way to tell unless you know the risk factor of both investment portfolios. The standard deviation will tell that. For instance, if portfolio A has a standard deviation of 10 while portfolio B has a 5, then portfolio B is better. It is safer than Portfolio A, so this is how the sharp ratio comes in handy to determine the risk factor/volatility of a certain stock. Ideally, it is good to have financial products with a higher sharp ratio.

This brings me to another point over here. Whenever the sharp ratio is higher than one, it is a good investment as we are taking the risk-reward ratio. Any investment under 1 means that the risk is too great, whereas its return is way too low. So, now, you have a good idea of how to go about investments, covering these bases.

Although previous performance is no guarantee of future returns, some historical numbers of the all-weather portfolio can tell about its history as a reliable and fail-safe financial product. For the previous three decades, the brainchild of Ray Dalio has delivered nearly eight percent returns (7.82%), whereas its standard deviation has been under seven (6.78).

When we compare S&P 500, its returns have been just below eleven percent (10.7%), while the standard deviation is fifteen percent (15%).

On this note, let us compare sharp ratios of both financial products:

The all-weather portfolio: 1.15

The S&P: 0.66

So, overall, the all-weather portfolio performs better if we look at the ratios here. However, if you are slightly younger and have some time on your hands, then you can manage higher volatility over time and can stand to gain more from pure stocks.

On the other hand, those in the above-50s age bracket or nearing retirement do not have much time at their end. This demographic cannot afford much volatility either. For them, Warren Buffet's rules are highly applicable:

Do not lose money

Always remember the first rule

In the previous chapter, I have shown how imperative it is to avoid losing money.

That is the rationale behind the all-weather portfolio by Ray Dalio. Essentially, four elements usually affect the asset value (which he accommodates in his brilliant portfolio):

Deflation

Inflation

Rising economic growth

Declining economic growth

Based on these factors, Dalio proposes that there will be four seasons of economic environments:

Inflation higher than expectations
Inflation that is lower than expectations

Economic growth that is higher than predictions

Economic growth that is lower than predictions

Dalio selected asset classes that perform better during these different economic cycles. In doing so, he creates a diversified portfolio that consistently grows despite carrying smaller downsides.

According to Dalio, losing less money is far more critical when the year is bad instead than chasing higher returns during a good year. This has been demonstrated abundantly with instances in the last chapter.

Listed below is the breakdown of the portfolio set up by Ray Dalio:

Thirty percent of U.S. stocks

Forty percent of long-term treasuries (bonds)

Fifteen percent of intermediate-term treasuries

Seven and a half percent commodities

Seven and a half percent gold

These are general rules.

However, exceptions are still there to this rule. For instance, stocks generally perform well when the market is rising. However, when the market underperforms, the stock's decline, but the deflation bonds remain stable in contrast. Under such struggling economic conditions, the interest rates take a nosedive. But then the interest rates and bond prices have an inverse relation. So, when the stock market underperforms, the rates go down, and bond prices go up.

But then the bigger question is how much it will go up? The answer largely depends on the term of the bonds in question. In short, when the interest rates drop, long-term bonds will skyrocket in contrast to intermediate- and short-term bonds. The same relation is vice versa as well. For instance, when the rates went up, the longer-term bonds suffered in contrast to the short term and intermediate-term bonds.

This is a good reason the all-weather portfolio performs well during economic recessions. For instance, when the S&P 500 had a shortfall of thirty-nine percent in 2008, the all-weather portfolio by Ray Dalio had a gain of nearly one and a half percent. The reason was that the long-term treasuries had a gain of nearly thirty-four percent (33.75%) while the intermediate-term bonds had a gain of thirteen percent (13.11%).

Another good instance is the three years while the "dot.com" bubble raged from 2000 to 2002. In this economic climate, the S&P 500 was down by these percentages:

9.10%
11.89%

22.10%

But the all-weather portfolio turned out to be the winner in this scenario. It posted returns of:

+10.15%

-2.77%

+7.77%

Thus, these historical figures openly present the strengths of this portfolio. It best serves the interest of people who require peace of mind and time horizon regarding their investments. In a typical scenario, the bonds and stocks will underperform when the economy is struggling, and the inflation rate is higher, with the economic activities becoming greatly limited. However, gold and commodities will work well in this climate.

Compare this year (as of June 2022) here when the inflation rate has been the highest for four decades. The overall portfolio was down by thirteen percent (13%) in June, whereas the S&P 500 was down by twenty-five percent (25%). As I write this chapter, the long-term bond was down by nearly twenty-five percent (24.6%), whereas IEI was down by nearly nine percent (9%).

But the commodities were up by nearly forty-three percent (43.5%), whereas gold (GLD) was up by under one percent (0.17%). So, we can see that gold underperformed more than expected. Despite gold's underperformance, the remainder of the portfolio exceeds the conventional stocks and bonds during this year of hyperinflation.

So, for those looking to create an all-weather portfolio, we can also create it independently. The trick is to use five low-cost ETFs to have a better-than-conventional balanced fifty-fifty stock and bond portfolio. This portfolio is easy to create and avoids the three percent advisory and management fees. Here is how you can do this:

30% VTI (Vanguard Total Stock market)

40% TLT

15% IEI

7.5% GLD

7.5% GSG

Since the time from 1973 to 2021, the decline has been only marginal these five years. Let us look here for a bit:

-3.74% in 1981

-3.28% in 1994

-2.77 in 2000

-3.72% in 2015

-3.19% in 2018

The decline has been over ten percent this year, but the odds of this occurring are even rare. For the past five decades, its highest loss in a year was only below four percent (3.74%).

This goes to show the consistency of the portfolio.

And now, as further proof, I will list down famous economic crises in this century, especially ones after 1973:

The OPEC oil price shock of 1973

Savings and loans crisis of the 1980s

Latin America Sovereign debt crisis of 1982

Stocks market crash of 1987

Junk bond crash of 1989

Tequila crisis 1994

Asia financial crisis of 1997 to 1998

Dotcom bubbles of 1999-2000 and then subsequently bear market

The global financial crisis of 2007 to 2008

The global pandemic of COVID-19 of 2020

Hyperinflation of 2022

From the above list of crises, one thing is pretty evident. We cannot, even the experts for that matter, predict any impending financial crisis and historical events. Similarly, no one can time the market with pinpoint accuracy either.

Anyone who attempts to time the market is probably playing poker with a poker champion—there is no way to win.

So, the obvious course of action is to focus more on the long-term horizon, dollar-cost averaging, steer clear of fees by

purchasing low-cost ETFs and allocate the money into a smartly designed all-weather portfolio. This portfolio will give decent enough returns provided it reduces the volatility. However, we should know one thing in this regard. Past performance is no guarantor of future returns. But there is more!

To sum it up, the understanding of financial products and investment options requires great discipline and patience. Great investors are trained to sit through the market's booms and busts before making a nice windfall.

Chapter 10
The Philosophy of Real Freedom

The premise of real freedom was coined by Philippe Van Parijs, a Belgian economist, and philosopher.

The concept talks about the idea of negative freedom by instituting institutional and other constraints on a person and choices. Aside from that, the model also adds resources, physical reality, and personal capacity into the mix.

Thus, according to Van Parijs, one can have freedom when these conditions are met:

- A person should be prevented from acting due to self-will (they should have conventional negative freedom).
- They should have the resources/capacities to carry their will
- Under this ambit, a person is free to take a holiday in some city since no one else is forcing them against this decision (the first condition is met)
- The person is not free to take a vacation since they cannot afford a flight (the second condition is unmet)

By this logic, people are negatively free to take a swim across the famed English Channel. However, they are not free because they lack swimming skills and would possibly drown even if they tried.

This implies that we are free to a certain degree, meaning that no one is categorically free. Thus, real freedom is a bridge too far for people because they satisfy one condition but find it difficult to satisfy another.

There should be a system/code of ethics that allows steering clear of this needless dynamic that has become part and parcel of our lives.

Concerns about one's financial situation are at the top of the list of the most frequently cited sources of stress, as shown by a survey conducted by the American Psychological Association (APA). It should not be shocking that so many people are affected by financial difficulties, given that these issues pose a direct risk to one's ability to preserve their own life. There is a wide range of severity in monetary issues' impact on our lives.

People's inability to pay their mortgages or maintain their homes is a common consequence of the financial difficulties that they experience. Even though they have to work hard to find food each day, there are still happy people in the world who are impoverished to the point where this is the case. Others are forced to sell their second vacation home in southern France because of a severe financial setback and dread the prospect of doing so. Therefore, the amount of stress we feel is partially determined by how we perceive the situation. Nevertheless, the Stoics have some sound advice to follow whenever we are in a stressful financial situation, regardless of the cause.

Ancient Stoics, who were closely affiliated with the school of the Cynics, did not place a high premium on amassing many material possessions. To them, time is more valuable than any other commodity. In addition, they considered our freedom of choice and action to be a much greater value than any money we might ever acquire. Having wealth certainly has its perks. However, this is not a prerequisite for experiencing joy in one's life. In order to survive, we require food and a place to sleep.

Moreover, this bare minimum is accessible to most of the world's population, even in the more impoverished regions of the globe. If you have bought this book, it is safe to assume that your fundamental requirements have been satisfied. On the other hand, it is usual for us to want more, regardless of how much we already possess. We want more on top of satisfying our fundamental requirements.

We are not interested in food; instead, we want delicious expensive food. We are not interested in clothing; instead, we are interested in designer clothing. We are not satisfied with merely having a roof over our heads; instead, we want a sizable home with several bedrooms, a garden, and a swimming pool. Therefore, to gratify our ever-increasing needs and wants, we require money—a great deal of it.

In addition, if we successfully attain a particular living level, we develop an attachment to that standard. Therefore, even though we still have plenty of financial resources to take care of the essentials, we become very agitated whenever there is a sudden change in the flow of money, such as when it goes from being completely open to almost entirely closed. So why can we not make do with less, at least temporarily? Is it because we want to appear successful compared to the Joneses? Exists within our social circle an environment that emphasizes one's status. Or is it possible that we are worried that those we care about will abandon us when we have no more money? According to Seneca, who is credited with saying, "Fidelity purchased with money, money can destroy," using wealth to entice romantic attachment is not a successful method. In addition, if we place an excessive amount of importance on wealth, it can be a significant contributor to unhappiness. Not only will we be afraid of being poor, but we will also have the sensation of being poor whenever we meet someone wealthier than us.

Living a stoic life does not entail that one lives a life without any material goods. As a matter of fact, the stoics feel that material goods are good to some extent since they allow us to live happily and virtuously. But their life does not revolve around as ours do.

That is because the Stoics are quite aware of consumerism's power over their decision-making and tranquility. We are often upset about not having a larger house or a better car. They fail to realize they have excellent health than so many other unfortunates out there and possessions far exceed others in comparison. Stoicism is hardly a novel concept.

As a matter of fact, Seneca freely practiced poverty, wearing unfashionable clothing to remind himself that material goods are unnecessary to lead a good life. He would also fast as well to show that he was like everyone else (the commoners) and could live satisfied in dire circumstances. Even though people have enough resources to live happily, unhappiness is always there since they want more from life. The insatiable desire is there to have more and more.

The stoics are satisfied with what they have and do not fret over their lacking. They are guided by awareness of their possessions and resources while also practicing gratitude.

The famed Roman Emperor Marcus Aurelius lived over two millennia ago. Even he, as a leader, staunchly believed in stoicism. The roman emperor commanding strength and massive power in geopolitics also had total control over the empire's resources. But his political ideals were vastly different at the time as a power broker in the European belt.

He famously once said:

"Almost nothing material is needed for a happy life for he who has understood existence."

The Roman emperor wielded great power at the time. However, he had little interest in the material world despite having the world at his feet. His internal world was all he had and something that he found more satisfying for the most part.

He believed in pursuing happiness, which he would accomplish by developing fortitude and virtue by living a stoic life. This would allow him to temporarily strip himself of the material things in life that seemed so important to live a good and balanced life. Marcus wished to show that he was above all this and strongly believed in the simple things in life.

For Marcus Aurelius, Stoicism was a handy framework to deal with life's stresses. After all, he was heading one of the most powerful empires of his day. He wrote the book "Meditations" during his life's last decade while campaigning against foreign invaders. Marcus openly embraced the studies of stoicism he had learned from his teachers. He also thanked his teachers, Rusticus and Epictetus, for influencing his life.

The tragedy is that his philosophy taught self-restraint, duty, and respect for others. However, it was abandoned abjectly during his time by the imperial line that he anointed.

We have come a long way since then, but some things never change. Back then, Marcus was taking a stand against materialism. However, we can see how much the times have changed!

Fast forward to this zeitgeist, materialism has taken a life of its own. Has it not? The times that Marcus saw in his lifetime have hardly changed.

The day we arrive in this world—we are thrown into this inexhaustible gamut of confusion, hunger, and vulnerability. Growing up then, we begin to accomplish material als/objectives in our pursuance to achieve higher social status and have money and fame. The aim is to have just enough to free ourselves of worldly pursuits, rat race, hardships, and emptiness.

The quest is to find optimum security and happiness in our lives, which becomes a vortex that takes a life of its own.

Despite the perspective itself, chasing money is not that unreasonable. However, it is no less a form of entrapment itself. We are trapped in a never-ending cycle of misery, nonetheless.

In order to understand the origin of unhappiness, we have to understand the importance of the following:

- Living frugally
- The sacrifice of saving money
- Psychological freedom
- These principles are a part of stoic philosophy

Zeno was a wealthy trader who lived in Cyprus city during 300 BC. While en route on a voyage from Phoenicia to Piraeus, his boat and the entire merchandise sank. This natural calamity was not on the cards, and as a result, Zeno became poor the moment the ship sank. How should one feel as a man who lost all his wealth in the sea? In the modern era, we have insurance and other facilities available at our disposal. The government even takes care of its people in some countries. This was not the case for Zeno, who was reduced to abject poverty almost immediately.

Someone like us would probably feel bad and blame divine powers and life for being unfair to us overall.

However, Zeno was indifferent to it. As the father of stoicism, he was above all material wealth. He merely shrugged as the last remnants of his wealth fell to the bottom of the oceans.

This was due to stoicism, which helped him keep calm and composure.

The Popularity of Stoicism

The philosophy is itself unique and has stood the test for thousands of years thus far. Interestingly, the teachings of stoicism are relevant now than it has ever been before. Its importance and application were not lost on others either. Many political and historical figures have understood and applied its principles over time. Famous proponents of stoicism include the likes of:

- Thomas Jefferson
- Eugene Delacroix
- George Washington
- Frederick the Great
- Walt Whitman
- Immanuel Kant
- Nelson Mandela
- Theodore Roosevelt
- Ralph Waldo Emerson
- Matthew Arnold
- Arthur Schopenhauer
- Ambrose Bierce
- Adam Smith

Stoicism is a viable philosophy since it helps instill resilience, presence, and calmness in a world that has become obsessed with materialism, greed, vanity, and a never-ending desire for more.

According to stoicism, we have an external and internal world.

- **External world:** This is the one we see all around us where we wield no control.
- **Internal word:** This is the one that harbors our subjective reactions and interpretations from looking at the world around us (external world).

The point is that when we pursue un innate things, we become engrossed in a future that holds no value since it rarely provides any inner satisfaction.

Basing our happiness on materialism and worldly possessions kickstarts a process beyond our control. It is like standing on a treadmill of desires, which fuels more desires initiating a loop.

As a result, we remain dissatisfied and unhappy because the loop is never-ending.

Now, I am not saying that chasing money is bad, nor is fame or power. These things are something that should be enjoyed in moderation. Even if they work out in some shape or form, it does not mean they are the key ingredients of life, fueling our happiness and peace of mind. We invite an element of inconsistency to the mix and become vulnerable.

The principle of stoicism establishes that a person should be perfectly fine with negating their desires, thus living a content life without them. Let us take a modern instance here.

Winston Churchill was a proponent of stoicism.

The man had invested a huge amount in the American stock exchange. This was during the 1920s when he suddenly lost £10,000 (which amounts to £500,000) overnight in the famously known event Black Thursday. The fateful event took place on October 24, 1929. Several people committed suicide that day. However, Winston Churchill was different in that regard. His response to the huge loss was as follows:

"Yes, how much better if I had spent it. What is money made for except to spend?" (Robert Andrew, Churchill page 388340).

There is a reason we should have a financially free lifestyle. This can happen by focusing on these simple elements:

- Real freedom
- A simpler lifestyle
- Minimalism
- Pursuing intellectualism
- Appreciate what we have already
- No comparison with others
- Subdue the unnecessary desires
- Living below the means

These are elements that we should control and focus on highly. However, we may need a framework to adopt these principles. Without a framework and a healthy understanding of stoicism, we can hardly make progress. Epictetus himself presented the model and strategies.

Epictetus was formerly a slave himself. However, he went on to become one of the most influential analytical thinkers in stoicism philosophy area. His book is titled *The Enchiridion*, which talks about implementing stoic principles in life. The man was talented at explaining the application of stoic strategies in life overall. He has talked at length regarding the viability of stoic principles in life, which have become renowned over time. His teachings have become famous, though credit sometimes alludes to him. One of the famous principles is the serenity prayer. This prayer goes something like this:

"God grant me the serenity to accept the things I cannot change, Courage to change the things I can, and wisdom to know the difference."

Lucius Annaeus Seneca (more popularly known as Seneca) was a Roman statesman and a famed stoic philosopher. He has famously stated:

"Until we have begun to go without them, we fail to realize how unnecessary many things are. We've been using them not because we needed them but because we had them."

This holds true even today. Though these famed words were spoken when the society was in a primitive stage, using capitalist models of that era.

Stoic philosophy's premise holds that freedom and happiness come from within instead of without. This means we should develop our character and perspective more than building material wealth and worldly possessions. Interestingly, nothing in life is good/bad. However, our perspectives, interpretations, and judgments of things may be good/bad.

Seneca writes:

"The wise man is neither raised by prosperity nor cast down by adversity; for always he has striven to rely predominately on himself and to derive all joy from himself."

In other words, spending effort to reach financial freedom is an easier, controllable way to serve best our ability to remain with long-lasting freedom, less anxiety, and consistent happiness. In a time where cultural pressure to live specific ways and achieve certain things overwhelm us 24/7, where we spend a considerable amount of time comparing ourselves to and wanting the approval of others, our level of happiness and freedom is increasingly fragile.

One of F. Scott Fitzgerald's short stories begins with the now-famous lines, "Let me tell you about the very rich. They are unique in comparison to both you and me. A few years after the publication of this story, Fitzgerald's friend Ernest Hemingway teased him by writing, "Yes, they have more money." Seneca is trying to get us to remember this fact. He was one of the wealthiest men in Rome, so he knew from personal experience that having more money does not significantly alter one's life.

People who do not have it appear to believe it will solve their problems, but it does not. No physical possession ever has. Things on the outside cannot fix problems on the inside. We consistently fail to remember this, which results in a great deal of muddle and suffering. In a later work, Hemingway would write about Fitzgerald: "He thought the rich were a glamorous special race, and when he found out they were not, it wrecked him as much as anything else." [Hemingway] ". If nothing is done differently, things will stay the same for us.

Warren Buffett, who has an estimated net worth of approximately $65 billion, still resides in the home he purchased in 1958 for $31,500. John Urschel, a lineman for the Baltimore Ravens, earns millions yearly but still only spends $25,000 on his living expenses. Even though he has a contract worth approximately $94 million, San Antonio Spurs star Kawhi Leonard still gets around in the 1997 Chevy Tahoe he has owned since he was a teenager. Why?

It is not because these guys have a low price point. It is because the things that are important to them do not cost much money. It was not by chance that Buffett, Urschel, or Leonard found themselves in this position. Their priorities have dictated the way they live their life. They devote their time and energy to pursuits that are unquestionably beneath their financial means; consequently, any income would give them the freedom to focus on the most important things. It was a total and ultimate fluke that they managed to amass an incredible fortune. They are now able to live their lives to the fullest because they have achieved such clarity regarding what it is in the world that they love the most. It indicates that they would be content despite adverse circumstances, such as an economic downturn or an injury that ended their careers prematurely. The more things we want and the more work we put in to earn or accomplish those goals, the less we enjoy our lives and the less freedom we have from those desires.

These are the types of people who should serve as examples for us. Seneca once said, "Without a ruler to do it against, you can't make crooked straight," and this maxim still holds today. In our lives, the role of wise people is to act as models for us to follow and to inspire us. So that we can run our ideas by them and check our assumptions, it is up to you to determine who that person will be for you. There is a chance it was either your dad or your mom. Perhaps it is a thinker, writer, or philosopher. Maybe it is all three. It is possible that following in Warren Buffet's footsteps is the best example for you to follow. Choose someone, such as the people I mentioned earlier, pay attention to what they do and do not do, and try as much as possible to model your behavior after theirs.

The system is rigged against us. We are constantly chasing a phantom that keeps eluding us. Would it not be better to catch the phantom in the act and call its bluff?

Now is the time to apply the principles of stoicism to assist ourselves in buying our ticket out of the rat race. Otherwise, we will be stuck in this cycle for the rest of our lives. We can work with stoicism and attain real freedom by using the money we are chasing round the clock. In doing so, we can also have more internal control and peace of mind.

Looking at the world around us, we see people frantically racing everywhere. Life is unsatisfactory, and the will to do more and have more rages on. The consumerist mindset is mechanical and formulaic, taking a life of its own when it gets attention.

The prevalent mindset is to have more material wealth and money to live the life one truly wants. We have this urgency to have a little more to have the desired future. The thought that having a bit more fame and fortune alongside power may bring us closer to true happiness keeps the cycle on repeat. Maybe tomorrow will be better than today, or maybe a few years down the line, we will live a life that we truly deserve.

This is how the consumerist mindset works!

It has pressurized us to have more and more. Everything should be in excess because less is more, yet more is never enough. This mindset has deluded us into thinking that true happiness lies in achieving material wealth and possessions, which may incur huge doses of stress and anxiety in our lives.

And when we do not have it, we are told it is perfectly fine. All we have to do is work harder to have those desired things. The more we work harder, the more things will unlock, and doors will open. As a result, we will buy more, possess more, and be happier.

This creates a never-ending feedback loop of consumerism—we are presently trapped with no way out.

So, normally, people follow three aims in life:
- Money
- Fame
- Freedom

The first two are solely related to our external world, which is something we do not control as much. The book's motive is to allow people to adopt and follow the third objective, freedom. When we follow financial freedom, we will essentially follow our internal desires. So, all we have to do is take control of our lives and finances into our hands.

When we control the time and finances, we are left to do things that make us happy and provide us with inner satisfaction. As a result, we can attain the highest form of happiness. That is the whole point of stoicism—taking control of the internal world and our happiness.

Let's sum it up with the most famous quote from the best renowned stoic philosopher Epictetus: "It is not what happens to you, but how you react to it that matters. There is only one way to happiness: to cease worrying about things beyond the power of our will. Wealth consists not in having great possessions but in having few wants. It is the nature of the wise to resist pleasures, but the foolish to be a slave of them."

As a result, stoicism is a good way forward to live our life. That is because the concept allows us to live the best possible life. Living by the stoicism code, we have the massive advantage of these traits:

- Declines negative emotions
- Maximizes positive emotions
- Allows an individual to hone their character virtues

This means that regardless of any phase of life, we can adopt stoicism in life. As is the case, stoicism provides a viable framework for living a good life. It helps remind people of the essential things in life and furnishes strategies to make life even more valuable.

Stoicism is easy to adopt—it is actionable, understandable, and valuable. Learning does not require adopting some philosophical lexicon or meditating for hours. It allows us to find tranquility, improve within ourselves, and improve our strength of character.

In short, the modern capitalist society has enslaved us into a rat race, initiating a cycle of consumerism and superficial pursuits. Stoicism provides a great way out of this cycle as it keenly focuses on self-development and happiness from within. It offers a much-needed exit strategy from the prevalent societal norms and social pressures.

In conclusion, we tend to ignore the things we already possess due to our preoccupation with the things we do not have. This is likely the case because we take so many things for granted and fail to recognize the many blessings we enjoy in our lives. Marcus Aurelius cautions us, however, not to become overly attached to things to the point where we would be 'upset' if we lost if we misplaced them.

Consequently, taking a Stoic stance on one's material possessions is a delicate process. On the one hand, we are to be content with what we have (and not desire what we do not have), but on the other hand, we are to strive to improve ourselves. However, we ought to have enough emotional distance from the things we possess so that the prospect of losing them will not bother us.

Chapter 11
The Power of Money

How about the song "Money"? What exactly is it? Furthermore, for what purpose is it? There are a variety of different manifestations that money can take. It is known to have taken the form of rocks, gems, gold, silver, and various other metals that were forged into various shapes, sizes, and weights in the past, and this practice is still practiced in some locations today. It has ranged from the claws of bears and sharks to shells, cigarettes, and even furs and bullets. Today, most people think of it as the various currencies used by the governments of different countries worldwide. Printed on textured, specialized paper with images of deceased presidents, the paper contains numbers meant to represent its value. Although all the items listed above and many more have served in the role of money at some point in history, none constitute "Money" on their own.

People are willing to work hard, pursue it, and even steal, cheat, and lie. Some people spend it, some save it, and some even worship it because of their love. Few can survive without it, and most of the world's population is a slave to it. However, very few people know what it is or what it is used for. Consider the so called "Dollar" bill, also known as the note, issued by the Federal Reserve today. What is the value of something if I spend a lifetime working for it, saving it, and then filling an entire room in my house with it until it reaches the ceiling? I cannot ingest it, I cannot put it on my body, nor can I construct a home out of it. It would have been challenging to maintain my body temperature by feeding a fire with it for more than a few nights. If that is the situation, why make such a big deal if you ask me? Even if we were still using bear claws, cigarettes, and bullets or fur, I am not sure whether I would be thrilled to have worked a lifetime for a room full of those items either; however, I could probably find more uses for them than I could for the colored paper. I do not know whether I would be thrilled to have worked a lifetime for a room full of colored paper.

Nowadays, "Money" can be stored as electronic bits, which are nothing more than a system of bookkeeping entries keeping track of credits and debits, offset mathematically with other credits and debits, and having no physical commodity at all called or representing the "Money" itself. The amount of a person's "Money" balance could be updated to reflect the value of their labor or the goods they produce, and this update could be done electronically as a numeric value. In this context, "money" refers to the difference between a person's credits and debits, and that person's "money" is the balance left over after those transactions. It makes no difference whether that balance is expressed in terms of dollars, bits, cents, or drachma as long as all participants in the transaction understand it. Although most people would be surprised to learn this, a piece of colored paper printed with the numeral one is not a dollar, even though it is so commonly referred to as a dollar.

Money is necessary and significant for some of us, but it is not the most important thing. It is nothing more than a tool, a source of power, and a life well lived when put to the service of others. Others are driven to such an extreme degree by their desire for wealth that it ruins them and everyone else in their lives. Some people are even willing to sacrifice much more valuable things to obtain it, such as their health, time, families, sense of self-worth, and in some cases, even their integrity.

Money is about power at its most fundamental level. We have all witnessed firsthand the transformative and destructive potential of monetary resources. It has the potential to either fund a dream or start a war. You can give someone money or use it as a weapon against them. It is possible to use it to express your spirit, creativity, and ideas; however, it is also possible to express your frustration, anger, and hatred. It is possible to use it to influence individuals as well as governments.

Some people get married for the wrong reasons and then learn the actual cost. However, we are all aware that this is, to some extent, an illusion. These days, money is not gold or paper; instead, it is represented as a series of zeros and ones in banking computers. What exactly is it? It is like a shapeshifter or a canvas in that it takes on the significance of feeling that is ascribed to it by the observer. In the end, we are not interested in pursuing a financial goal, correct? We are not after the material things; we want the feelings and the emotions that we believe money can give us.

One of the ways that we can make the dreams we have into the reality that we live is most certainly through the use of money. If you do not have enough of something, it does not feel like it is just a perception or an abstract concept, even if that is what money is. You either make use of it, or it uses you; there is no middle ground. Either you have control over money, or money has control over you on some level!

This is how money gives you power or how you can master money. How much of a return can you expect on the money you have saved up in the bank if it enables you to switch careers, retire earlier, or live your life worry-free? I would say it is unmeasurable. It is impossible to calculate in two different ways. Because of its magnitude and significance, we cannot place a monetary value on it. However, in addition to that, it is impossible to calculate; we cannot measure it in the same way that we measure interest rates, and things that we are unable to measure are frequently ignored. When you do not have command over your time, you have no choice but to make the most of the unfortunate circumstances that befall you. However, if you are flexible, you will have the time to wait for opportunities that are a no-brainer to take advantage of when they present themselves. This is a return on your savings that you did not expect. If you have the flexibility to take a job with a lower salary but more purpose, or if you can wait for investment opportunities that come when those without flexibility turn desperate, then savings in the bank that earn 0% interest could generate an excellent return for you.

How would you feel if you did not have to worry about going to your workplace every morning, paying the bills, or funding your retirement? How would you feel? What would it be like to live according to the rules you set for yourself? What would it mean to you if you knew that you had the opportunity to start your own business, that you could afford to buy a home for your parents and send your kids to college, or that you could have the freedom to travel the world? How would you live your life if you knew that there would be enough money every morning when you woke up to cover your essential requirements and your long-term objectives and desires? The fact is that most of us are hardwired in such a way that we would continue to be employed.

Nevertheless, we would do it from a place filled with joy and abundance. Our labor would be ongoing, but we would no longer have to compete against one another. Instead of working because we are required to, we would work because we want to.

The most crucial factor to creating wealth and becoming financially free is to become a master of thrift. However, the big spenders are sensationalized and promoted by the popular press for an excessive amount of time. The media never stops pumping us full of hype about athletes who are supposedly worth millions of dollars. There is some truth to the rumor that some people who make up this relatively small population are millionaires. If, on the other hand, a highly skilled ball player makes $5 million a year, then having a net worth of $1 million is not a big deal at all. According to our formula for calculating wealth, a person who is thirty years old and makes $10 million per year should have a net worth of at least $30 million. How many professional ball players make a high salary and have a level of wealth that falls within this range? We only believe a tiny portion of it. Why? Because most of them live an extravagant lifestyle, which they can maintain so long as they make a substantial amount of money each year. On paper, they might be millionaires (having a minimum net worth of at least one million dollars or more). However, statistically speaking, they are not exceptionally high on the scale of prodigious accumulators of wealth.

However, a great way of life is good for ratings on TV stations and circulation in newspapers. Young people are taught all too frequently that "those who have money spend lavishly" and "if you do not show it, you do not have it" (if you do not show it, people will assume you do not have it). Could you even fathom the media making a big deal about how frugally the average American millionaire lives their life? What kind of outcomes could we anticipate? Low TV ratings and a lack of leadership can be attributed to the fact that most people who build wealth in the United States work hard, save money, and are not glamorous. One rarely gets rich by winning the lottery, hitting a home run, or performing well on a game show. However, these are the extremely rare jackpots sensationalized by the media.

Many people in the United States can manage increases in their realized income, particularly those who fall into the category of being under accumulators of wealth. They put them to use! Their desire for satisfaction right away is powerful. They see life as something akin to a game show. Winners are awarded immediate cash as well as noticeable prizes. The audience members of these game shows feel great compassion for the contestants. Look at the high ratings that these shows consistently receive. People take great pride in showing off their surrogate winners, whether a motor vehicle, boat, appliance, or money. Why don't television game shows give away scholarships to college as prizes? Because most people crave instant gratification. Even though earning a college degree can translate into a value equivalent to more than a dozen vans, they do not want to give up a prize of something like a camper van to spend eight years attending night classes.

In the 1970s, widespread concern was that the world would soon run out of oil. It was not hard to calculate: the global economy used much oil, the global economy was growing, and the amount of oil we could drill for could not keep up with the growing demand. Thankfully, we were able to avoid running out of oil. However, this was not only because we discovered additional oil or even became more proficient at extracting it from the ground. The most critical factor in our success in overcoming the oil crisis is that we began producing automobiles, factories, and homes that are more energy efficient than they were in the past. When measured against its GDP, the United States now consumes sixty percent less energy than it did sixty years ago. Since 1975, the number of miles traveled on a single gallon of gas has more than doubled. The 1989 Ford Taurus sedan got an average of 18.0 miles per gallon. The 2019 Chevrolet Suburban, an absurdly large SUV, gets 18.1 miles per gallon on average.

The world's "energy wealth" increased not due to an increase in the amount of energy it possessed but rather due to a reduction in the required energy. Since 1975, oil and gas production in the United States has increased by 65%, and thanks to improvements in efficiency and conservation, the amount of work that can be done with that energy has more than doubled. Therefore, it is not hard to determine which has been of greater significance. The most important aspect of this situation is finding more energy is primarily outside of our control and shrouded in uncertainty. This is because finding more energy depends on a complex mixture of suitable geology, geography, weather, and geopolitics. However, we have much control over how much more efficiently we can use the energy we consume. You are the only person who can determine whether riding a bike or purchasing a car that weighs less will result in a more significant improvement in efficiency.

The same is true about our monetary resources. Returns on investments have the potential to make you wealthy. However, there is always the possibility that a particular investment strategy will not work, that it will work for only a limited amount of time, or that markets will not cooperate. A cloud of doubt surrounds the findings. Personal savings and frugality, also known as the conservation and efficiency of finance, are aspects of the money equation that are more directly under your control and have a one hundred percent chance of being just as effective in the future as they are right now. You risk becoming as pessimistic about your ability to build wealth as the energy doomers were in the 1970s if you view wealth creation as something that will require more money or significant investment returns. The way forward appears to be challenging and beyond your control. Destiny becomes much clearer when viewed as something powered by your thriftiness and efficiency. Wealth is simply the accumulated remainder left over after one has spent what they have brought in. Moreover, because it is possible to amass wealth without having a high income, but there is no possibility of doing so without having a high savings rate, it is obvious which factor is more important.

Unfortunately, the reality is ruthless. Only forty percent of Americans report having any spending or investment plan, even though seventy-seven percent of them, or three out of every four, say they are concerned about their financial situation. One in every three members of the baby boomer generation has less than $1,000 stashed away. Not even one in four people believe the financial system can be trusted, and there is a good reason for that. Moreover, the number of people who own stocks has been reaching record lows, especially among younger people. However, the reality is that there is no path to freedom that involves earning it.

Even multimillion-dollar earners like Godfather director Francis Ford Coppola, boxer Mike Tyson, and actress Kim Basinger lost it all because they did not apply the fundamentals we have discussed in this book. You need to be able to save some of what you earn for your loved ones and multiply what you earn so that you are making money even while you are sleeping. You have to transition from being a consumer in the economy to becoming an owner, and the way to do that is to become an investor. This is the only way to make the transition. The famous book *The Richest Man In Babylon* illustrates the five laws of gold:

1. Gold cometh gladly and in increasing quantity to any man who will put by not less than one-tenth of his earnings to create an estate for his future and that of his family.

2. Gold laboreth diligently and contentedly for the wise owner who finds profitable employment, multiplying even as the field flocks.

3. Gold clingeth to the protection of the cautious owner who invests it under the advice of men wise in its handling.

4. Gold slippeth away from the man who invests it in businesses or purposes with which he is unfamiliar, or which are not approved by those skilled in its keep.

5. Gold flees the man who would force it to impossible earnings, followeth the alluring advice of tricksters and schemers, or trusts it to his own inexperience and romantic desires in investment.

The conclusion that can be drawn from these five laws is that people who become masters of money organize their time, energy, and financial resources in a manner that is congruent with increasing their net worth. When it comes to how much time they spend on wealth-building activities, people who are prodigious and under-accumulate wealth have entirely different perspectives. Although both types of people have similar goals for achieving wealth, when it comes to how much time they spend on wealth building activities, these groups have entirely different perspectives.

Here is one of the great stories that show what saving diligently and living frugally means to the beautiful side of money. Osceola McCarty came into this world in 1908 and had a difficult beginning in her life. She was conceived as a result of her mother being sexually assaulted on a path through the woods in rural Mississippi on her way back from tending to a sick relative. Osceola was brought up in Hattiesburg by her grandmother and aunt, who were housekeepers, cooked, and did laundry in addition to their other responsibilities.

When Osceola was a young girl, she would come home from elementary school, iron clothes, and put the money she made into her doll buggy. The three women were utterly dependent on one another. When one of the women's aunts returned from a hospitalization unable to walk, Osceola dropped out of sixth grade to care for her and take a job as a washerwoman. She never went back to finish her education. As a result, she spent most of her life—that is, 75 years—ironing and washing clothes. The most incredible thing about her was that she kept a low-key lifestyle and consistently put some of her income into savings.

This washerwoman had been paid her entire life in small piles of coins and dollar bills; however, by the time she retired in 1995, she had accumulated a savings account balance of $280,000 despite suffering from painfully swollen hands caused by arthritis.

McCarty put aside just enough money to cover her living expenses before donating $150,000 to the University of Southern Mississippi to fund scholarships for deserving but financially disadvantaged students seeking the education that McCarty did not have. As soon as people in Hattiesburg and the surrounding area learned about what she had done, over 600 different men and women increased her endowment by more than three times its previous value. Today, the university offers several McCarty scholarships that cover the recipient's total tuition costs annually.

Suppose money is indeed a tool and a source of power. Then, Oseola McCarthy decided to use this power even though it would reduce her standard of living to assist those who could not pay for the education she had always yearned for but could not obtain.

The way to financial freedom, the art of mastering your money, and the pursuit of happiness are living humbly, saving diligently, and investing correctly. We will conclude the chapter and the book with the story of a janitor named Ronald Read to illustrate these central themes of this book. The death of Ronald Read occurred when he was 92 years old. The man from Brattleboro, Vermont, who had not attended college and drove a Toyota Yaris, made it a point to live below his means throughout his entire life consistently. After several years as an attendant at a gas station, he spent the remainder of his career working as a janitor for the J.C. Penney department store in his hometown.

Read exemplified the academic research conducted by men such as the late Dr. Thomas J. Stanley of the University of Georgia and Dr. Jeremy J. Siegel, a professor at Wharton. Read was a near-perfect archetype of their work. Like most Americans in the top 1 percent of wealth, Ronald was stealthy about it, keeping his money a secret from his children and friends. This is because Ronald was in the top 1 percent of the wealth. After he passed away, they were surprised to learn that he had a safe deposit box containing a stack of stock certificates that were five inches thick. However, they were aware that he had a passion for investing.

This was in addition to the nearly a dozen and a half direct stock purchase plans in which he was enrolled via electronic registration. He did this to take advantage of the lower costs that these plans offered now that ordering out physical stock certificates is costly. Read also kept a small amount of money in a brokerage account, representing a relatively insignificant portion of his overall holdings.

The estate, with the assistance of Wells Fargo & Company, is currently tallying up his holdings and attempting to determine the scope of his fortune; however, as of their most recent count, they are aware that he owned at least 95 businesses that have a combined market value of $8,000,000. On top of his roughly $12 an hour job, he was probably pulling down more than $20,000 a month in dividend income before taxes. This assumes that the weighted assets had a dividend yield of 3 percent.

His largest stock positions were:

Wells Fargo & Company = $510,900

Procter & Gamble = $364,008
Colgate-Palmolive = $252,104

American Express = $199,034

J.M. Smucker = $189,722

Johnson & Johnson = $183,881

VF Corp. = $152,208

McCormick = $145,055

Raytheon = $142,970

United Technologies = $140,880

You may recall some recommendations I made regarding investment rules in chapter 8 to consistently put money into large, well-known businesses with a proven track record of business success over a prolonged period. They need to have a high entry barrier to assist you in adhering to Warren Buffet's investment rules, which state that you should never lose money. It should be no surprise that Read's investment portfolio was utterly consistent with these ideas.

What was his secret to financial success?

He got his feet wet slowly. The Wall Street Journal states that the trades can be traced back to the 1950s and had a humble beginning. They offer one illustrative example. On January 13, 1959, when he was around 37 years old, he purchased 39 Pacific Gas & Electric shares for $2,380. This transaction has an inflation adjusted total value of approximately $19,200 in today's purchasing power equivalent.

He has spent the past sixty years and some change working stealthily, patiently, and consistently to amass equity in some of the most successful companies in the world, spanning various business sectors. He was the owner of railroads, banks, credit card companies, credit card companies, industrial conglomerates, dish soap and toothpaste empires, packaged food giants, and just about anything else you can think of. It did not matter to him that there were multiple wars, inflation, deflation, numerous changes in the tax code, or the threat of nuclear annihilation; he just kept plugging away at it with discipline, acquiring more ownership of productive assets despite all these things. His portfolio value would have dropped by 50 percent or more on paper multiple times, but he kept plugging away at it.

He would only invest in companies he had personal experience with and knew well enough to make informed decisions. He would only invest in companies that would pay him a dividend because he wanted to be able to physically watch the check arrive in the mail. He would then deposit the check and use the money it contained to purchase additional company shares to expand the passive income he received each month.

He was like the highly wealthy Vanguard clients that John Bogle describes, who invest in individual stocks but do not sell anything they own. He avoided turnover as much as possible, opting for holding periods that spanned multiple decades. This gentleman was the definition of a buy-and-hold investor. He was aware of the risks associated with activity, the positive aspects of paying taxes later, and the wealth eroding effects of paying excessive fees.

For example, he had a stake in Lehman Brothers, which was wiped out during the Great Recession of 2008-2009; he continued to hold onto his shares even though the company had declared total bankruptcy. This demonstrates that he had a solid understanding of the mathematical principles behind diversification. He relied on an intelligently constructed, diversified, and representative list of common stocks arranged so that the inevitable losses were overshadowed by the growth and income of the other holdings. He diversified his holdings across a wide range of industries and companies.

Even more astonishing is that Read seems to have been driven, at least partly, by altruism. He left nearly all his wealth to charitable causes, including legacies for a regional medical facility and the public library he frequently visited for research investments.

The findings of more recent studies have demonstrated that having more money can increase one's level of happiness. "Spending five dollars a day change your happiness," according to the findings of various scientific studies. How so? How one spends their money is more important than the total amount spent. "Everyday spending choices unleash a cascade of biological and emotional effects that are detectable right down to saliva," While having more money can provide all kinds of beautiful things— from tastier food to safer neighborhoods—its real power comes not in the amount but in how we spend it.

According to numerous pieces of research, the more you help other people, the happier you will feel. Furthermore, the more you have, the more you can give away. It is a circle of goodness if you will. According to Dunn and Norton's research in the field of science, individuals report higher happiness levels when they donate money to charitable causes rather than spending it on themselves. The advantages "do not only extend to one's subjective well-being but also one's objective health." Giving to others makes you happier and better for your health.

Spending money to buy more control over your time and freedom will not only make you happier. However, it will also improve your physical health because a lack of control over one's time can have a profound and widespread impact on one's level of happiness. The highest dividend that can be earned in finance is the ability to do whatever you want, whenever you want, with whomever you want, and for as long as you want.

The most effective step to improve your results as an investor is to broaden the time horizon over which you make decisions. When it comes to investing, time is the most critical factor. It magnifies the insignificant while diminishing the significance of the significant. Although it cannot eliminate the effects of chance and danger, it brings results that align with what individuals deserve. It would help if you also exercised extreme caution regarding the costs associated with investing. Be careful not to fall into the trap that will cause you to lose money by forcing you to pay unnecessary and expensive fees.

Let us end it with Steve Jobs's quote:"

Being the richest man in the cemetery does not matter to me. Going to bed at night saying we have done something outstanding is what matters to me

www.ingramcontent.com/pod-product-compliance
Lightning Source LLC
Chambersburg PA
CBHW052350220526
45465CB00003BA/1046